G000123143

Downhill to the Top

The world's first woman to ski every continent:
Guinness Record

Downhill to the Top

Norma Rowlerson

with her illustrations

© Norma Rowlerson 2008

Published by Northern Press 2008

ISBN 978-0-9558734-0-9

Norma Rowlerson has asserted the right under the Copyright, Designs and Patents Act 1988 to be identified as the author of the book.

All rights reserved. Reproduction of this book by photocopying or electronic means for non-commercial purposes is permitted. Otherwise, no part of this book may be reproduced, adapted, stored in a retrieval system or transmitted by any means, electronic, mechanical, photocopying, or otherwise without the prior written permission of Norma Rowlerson.

Cover prepared by Clare Brayshaw

Set in Century Old Style 10.5/13pt

Prepared and printed by:
York Publishing Services Ltd
64 Hallfield Road
Layerthorpe
York YO31 7ZQ
Tel: 01904 431213
Website: www.yps-publishing.co.uk

For Jonathan

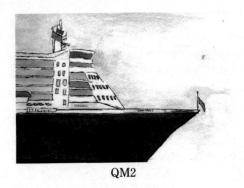

QM2

Chapter One

Two men looked out through prison bars,
one saw mud, the other stars.

'If there is a precipice ahead, I'll be mincemeat.' This was the thought which flashed through my head as I crashed down the icy piste at breakneck speed, executing six somersaults as I went.

At 51, skiing was new to me. I had bought the cheapest ski trousers I could find as I had thought that I might not take to the sport. They were shiny black and so slippery that I might as well have been hurtling down the slope on a tin tray. I had heard that ski guides in India, having led their clients up the mountain, would then whizz down sitting on Teachers' whisky tin trays wearing just wisps of cotton clothing. I suddenly knew the feeling.

The day had started well as I zapped along in the sunshine with the group of skiers. We were led by Herman, a stocky, wiry ski instructor who lived in the small Austrian village. His main job was farming but when the snows came he switched from his rural role and assumed the mantle of ski guru. He mixed effortlessly

1

with jet setters from all over the world who hung on his every word.

At the point of my dramatic descent we were crossing ice and I had not mastered edging. I slipped and fell on the glass-like surface, facing up the mountain with my skis crossed behind me. What a nightmare.

All it took was the slightest movement, just the twitch of a muscle, to set me off. As I careered down, I was briefly halted by a violent bang on the back of my head. But this was not enough to stop my progress and off I set again. It turned out afterwards that my head had hit the ski of a Swedish dentist who was on his honeymoon. He emerged unscathed and so did his ski. He told me afterwards that he was horrified as he watched me hurtle by, powerless to help.

I knew that it would be curtains for me if I reached a sheer drop and I rued the day that I had begun to ski. Abruptly my awful journey came to an end. I opened my eyes and the scene was like an abattoir. I had landed on a little plateau and there was blood, mine, everywhere. Shaken and tearful, I looked up. The rest of the class had gathered round and gazed down at the mess. I pleaded with the instructor to send for the Blood Wagon. This is a sort of wheeled stretcher used to bring casualties down the mountain. But having checked me over to ensure I had broken no bones, he insisted that I skied down behind him. In fact I felt better for being straight back on skis, although flecks of my blood flew into the air as I moved.

We went into a mountain restaurant so that I could clean myself up. Other skiers lounging in the sunshine looked shocked when they saw our little procession. I saw why when I looked in a mirror. Blood had streamed down my face and had soaked into my white polo neck, turning it scarlet. After a short break, we skied on down and I went into the doctor's surgery, conveniently situated at

2

the base of the slopes. I was given eight stitches to a gash in the back of my head and left wearing a huge turban of white bandage.

I clomped back to the hotel disconsolately wondering what to do with myself for the rest of the week. I spent an uncomfortable dinner in the restaurant, feeling self conscious about the bandage.

However, I was not concussed and the next day the doctor removed the bandage. He told me that I was allowed to return to the slopes if I took it gently. I felt fine. The back of the head is one part of the body that can be stitched and yet not interfere with skiing.

At the end of the week I made a more controlled descent of the Valluga, a fearsome slope. It is reached by a lift which hauls you across space and then deposits you on a tiny ledge, like an eyelash protruding from the mountain. My hat slipped as I got out of the lift, revealing the stitches through a gauze dressing and drawing comment from an Austrian man: 'The hardy British.'

My motto in life is simple. I never say 'No' because I believe that life is for living, so I will try anything once. I have had more than my fair share of adventures and experiences after adopting this approach.

Optimism is a great asset. I have a tendency to see the glass as half full and my confidence is rewarded when I set my mind to overcome a challenge and usually find there is a way to achieve whatever goal it is that I have set myself.

Who would have guessed that my late start in skiing would lead to my being a travel writer and to appear in the Guinness records as the first woman to ski every continent?

Like a lot of lucky breaks, beginning to ski came by chance. As we would have been alone at home with our son one Christmas, we decided to go abroad. By then it was too late to find rooms in any sun-spot. The only accommodation available was in an Austrian village. We had no intention of skiing. When the transfer bus spiralled up a snowy road to the resort I thought that I had landed in Paradise.

My love affair with snow had begun as a child in Canada. Perhaps my winter birthday had given me a predilection for icy climes. A happy memory of the three-year wartime separation from my parents is of looking out of the window and watching snowflakes the size of half crowns floating silently down past the street lights. Togged up in a hand-me-down snow suit, I would be off to the park the next day to hurtle down a slope on a toboggan. Subsequently, my cousin lent me a pair of his out-grown ice hockey skates. I optimistically took to the ice. The outdoor 'rink' at the park was flooded by hose pipe each night so there was always a perfect new surface the following day. I still remember the agony of learning to skate: the low cut boots gave no support. My ankles were weak. Barely able to stand, I went around the ice mostly on the sides of the outsize boots. But the baptism of fire eventually paid off and I was able to skate reasonably well but was never a match for the local children who had skated all their lives. In 1947, the UK's exceptionally cold winter especially in the north was my first experience of British skating. The local mere in Cheshire froze for many weeks. Christmas holidays were extended by several weeks as pipes in schools and barracks were frozen and many had burst. We had the time of our lives, cycling or driving a few miles to Booth Mere and spending blissful days there skating for many hours.

The King's Coffee House in Knutsford (Cranford in fiction) was a haven for lunches. Run by elderly twins, the subject of their conversation was almost as rich as the warming food. As suffragettes, they had chained themselves to the Home Office railings. Subsequently arrested, they were forcibly fed. I never fail to think of them at election times. Cheshire women would have been inspired by Mrs. Pankhurst, born in nearby Manchester.

There did not seem much to do in the Austrian village so we joined the throng on the way to the ski hire shop. I took to skiing from the start.

On our return home, Mary Quant said to me that if I liked the sport and could do it, I should go back again that same season and consolidate my progress. This I did. Skiing is possibly one of the few holidays which you can take alone and not feel out of place. Once in the resort, joining the ski school provides built-in playmates for the whole time. After a day of strenuous exercise, all that is needed is a hot bath, a good dinner and an early night in order to be ready for the following day.

My original ambition to be a journalist was about to materialise. The wartime education in Canada had disrupted my education and put paid to any hopes of writing as a career. Like most Scots, my father believed that whatever one's eventual job, be it as a surgeon or a plumber, you must be properly trained. He and most of his siblings were graduates of Aberdeen University. My Aunt Elisabeth must have been quite a pioneer, graduating as an MA in English in 1908. She was a teacher in her home town, Montrose, for many years and roared the roads of Angus on a motorbike. One day, she met a former pupil in the High Street. The pupil, pushing a pram which was brimming with babies, called out merrily: 'Hello, Miss Grieve, do you remember me? You learnt me English?'

My brother had graduated from school in Canada which automatically took him to Oxford. No exams were involved – it was a process of continuous assessment. I was three years behind. When I returned home I was dismayed to be told that plans had been made for me to board at St.Leonard's School in St.Andrews, Scotland. I was shocked that my parents were going to send me away again. I robustly refused to go. Instead I became a day girl at a local school. My mother said that I would regret it all my life. I have never regretted it for a moment.

For a year after our return, I was coached every evening in French, Algebra and Geometry, none of which had been on the Canadian curriculum. History and Geography had focused mainly on Canada so I was coached in those subjects as well. On Saturday mornings, I would cycle some distance to be taught Latin. This was provided by a retired headmaster cum parson. I would hurl my Famous James bicycle against the wall of the vicarage and make my way into the gloomy interior. Dr. Veerman looked like Methusala to me and he had married a woman much older than himself. They were childless. His wife was not prepared to leave him alone with any female, even as gauche a schoolgirl as I was then. So she lay on a chaise lounge in the study with us, smoking endlessly. I spent most of the time counting the pictures which hung on every inch of the walls. Sometimes Mrs Veerman would fall asleep, the cigarette dropping onto her clothes. The lessons were thus enlivened when I had to distract Dr. Veerman from his dry diatribes and shout: 'Dr. Veerman, Dr. Veerman, your wife's on fire!'

My family wanted me to follow my brother's example and go up to Oxford, but by then I had had enough studying and was not prepared to do any more. I still wanted to be a journalist. But my father was insistent that I have some further education. It never occurred to me to defy my parents, to leave my comfortable home, find somewhere to live and find a job as a journalist. Estrangement and starving in a garret never entered my head. Maybe I was just being realistic: what would I have lived on before I found a job ?

Whatever the reasons for the delay, when I did take up my pen to earn money it was heady stuff. I never looked back.

On leaving school, I went off to Edinburgh and became a Home Economist. During my last term, a Demonstrating Course was introduced. Not only were our cooking skills honed but we attended a school of speech and drama to brush up on presentation. This I loved and I have always enjoyed connecting with an audience.

Going to Canada came about because of World War Two. My parents decided to send my brother and me across the Atlantic for safety as my mother's brother lived in Toronto. In the summer of 1939, before the outbreak of war, we went on a family holiday to Canada and the USA. It was then that my uncle told my father to send us to him in the eventuality of war breaking out. The final excitement of the holiday was a visit to the World's Fair in New York. Then we were to sail home on the Queen Mary. It was interesting recently to tour her successor, QM2.

In the weeks leading up to WW2, the whole complexion of the eagerly anticipated voyage changed as war was imminent. Our trip turned out to be the ship's last peacetime voyage from New York to Southampton. We were told that potentially enemy ships, the Bremen and Europa were both armed and that one was sailing ahead of us and the other behind. Had war broken out whilst we were at sea, there is little doubt that the intention was to blow the Queen Mary out of the water. Our ship was unarmed. Blacked out from the start, we fairly raced across the ocean; stabilisers were not fitted at that time and the crossing was very rough. The ship broke her own peacetime record. We arrived at Southampton just days before war broke out. Although I was only ten, my memories of the holiday are still vivid. The experience has been kept fresh in my mind as my father recorded the holiday on colour 8mm film, now magically transferred to video.

The next year my parents sent my brother and me back to Toronto. There was a very real threat that Britain would be invaded. I never resented their sending us away. They saw us off at Liverpool in June 1940 on the Duchess of Atholl, having given me a gold locket with their photographs inside. My father came into my bedroom the night before we sailed and said that I had to be brave the next day, for my mother's sake.

My brother and I shared a passport, my photograph pasted into the space for 'Wife/Femme.' My brother's signature is there but presumably I was deemed too young to sign. There is a later endorsement for our eventual trip home which reads 'No time to make enquiries.' We were sailing in convoy but rarely saw our escort. On the Sunday, the Captain took a religious service in the ship's lounge. Thinking that attending was the right thing to do, I donned my beret and went. When we sang:'For those in peril on the sea' I thought, 'That's us!'

It took almost three years for it to become apparent that Britain would not after all be invaded. It was a curious time. It was not then possible to send any money abroad so there was a financial burden on the hosts. We children were aware of this. The private school to which I went waived the fees for 'War Guests' as we were called. There was no telephoning, no e-mail. Just letters which came by sea and were sometimes censored. They were bleak days emotionally.

On my twelfth birthday, my mother sent this poem with presents:

Today my Norma is twelve years old
And though so far away
I wish her joy and fun untold
On this her happy birthday.

A Fair Isle scarf for you I've knitted
In colours bonny and gay
I hope it keeps my wee lass warm
Throughout many a day.

Dad has sent you a handbag green
The bonniest one I have ever seen
Our loving thoughts go out to you
Across the rolling ocean blue.

I still have the scarf.

Then the wonderful day came when it was time for us to come back to Britain. My brother was approaching the military call-up age of eighteen. My father thought it preferable for him to join the British rather than the Canadian army. If we returned to England before he went into the army, he would be able to study for a short time at Oxford first. This would ensure a more rapid readmission for him after the war, a Z release as it was called.

Our journey home began in February 1943, right in the middle of the Battle of the Atlantic. The only way for unaccompanied British children and for most civilians to cross the Atlantic was on a ship from a neutral country. One such was the Serpa Pinto, a Portuguese vessel. That trip seemed to mark the start of a new life for me. I was at last on my way home.

Sailing from Philadelphia, we called in at Bermuda and the Azores before landing at Lisbon. We were fortunate. On a trip soon afterwards, the Serpa Pinto was stopped by a German U-boat and the ship's affable doctor was drowned during the exercise. It was said that they were looking for British boys of military age. The many notables on each trip no doubt attracted attention too. One of our companions was a god-daughter of the Duke of Kent, accompanied by her nanny. Nanny was going home to marry a policeman, then stationed at Buckingham Palace.

The plan was that we would fly from Lisbon to England. Our flight was delayed because the route was much in demand. BOAC's archives reveal that Churchill called it 'Lifeline.' It was considered dangerous and indeed it was. The plane carrying the actor Leslie Howard was lost on the same route and its fate remains a mystery. Our stay in Lisbon eventually lasted for a month and was full of interest.

All our travel arrangements were made by Thos. Cook, who at that time acted as agents for the government. Their representative came to our Lisbon hotel every day and gave us as much money as we wanted. This we spent on sightseeing to Mont Estoril, where we had lived as infants. I was growing fast so I bought a whole new wardrobe. I had a suit made, bought blouses handsewn by nuns, new shoes and much else. I felt smart and quite grown up.

As the capital of a neutral country, Lisbon was frequented by all nationalities. When I was wearing a tartan skirt one day, I was spat at by a Japanese man. He passed quickly in the crowd. Shaken, I wiped the saliva off my cheek. But I was not surprised as I was, after all, his enemy. Our hotel seemed to be a sanctuary for young British pilots who had been shot down in France and had then walked into neutral Portugal. From there they were spirited home. A fellow traveller reminded me recently that one of them arrived late one night in a bloodstained uniform greatcoat. He had no apparent injuries. The older boys rigged him out in their civilian clothes and they all went out on the town. He was young and handsome but had gone by the following morning.

When we eventually reached the UK, my father, despite his delight upon seeing us, was rather taken aback by the large bill which came from Thos. Cook. He said to me, in his gentle Scottish way, 'Now, lass you will sit down and write about where you have been.' This I did on the same Underwood typewriter on which he had written prewar reports from Spain and Portugal for ICI and on which, long afterwards, I wrote my first articles.

The rather naïve account of our journey home retraces most of the trip. I had enjoyed English lessons and writing essays at school and carried a small dictionary in my pocket. This is the only record that has survived.

Having flown to UK from Lisbon, my brother and I were taken to Bristol station in an RAF car where we were put on a train north. As petrol was scarce, my parents met us in a taxi at Alderley Edge station in Cheshire. It was dark and my mother was wearing a brimmed felt Henry Heath hat in a heathery colour. She was always stylish. I was shocked when I saw in the dim light that there was a streak of white hair across her forehead, although the remainder was still very dark. I did not feel estranged from her and soon settled back into a happy home. She rarely mentioned her life after we had gone away. One exception was when she told us of a Christmas Day without us. Many soldiers were stationed in nearby houses which had been requisitioned. Ours was open house for baths and general R&R. My mother said that she had visited some soldiers one Christmas Day, no doubt taking goodies with her. They eventually said to her that she should get home to her children. She had replied that her children were in

Canada. She did not elaborate – perhaps it was too painful for her.

I saw the Douglas plane in the Transport Museum in Brussels on a later press trip. There has been speculation about Leslie Howard's doomed journey. On a Radio Four programme subsequently it was suggested that passengers on that route were issued with parachutes and that descending figures were seen. I was able to question this theory as there were no parachutes on our plane. Another suggestion was that the falling figures were women with their skirts billowing out around them.

As planned, my brother went up to Oxford to read Law before joining up. He did a year's work in one term and also captained the university Chess team. He was a tough act to follow.We watched his degree ceremony from the gallery in the Radcliffe Camera, Oxford, my mother and I wearing hats, gloves and Dior 'New Look' suits. My brother was the only candidate to be capped in his discipline so he was led by hand up to the governing body by a tutor on each side. All names were translated into Latin. His, Valentine Grieve, translated well, his first name coming from our paternal grandmother who was of Huguenot descent.

I spent three years as a cookery demonstrator. This was long before the days of Fanny Craddock, never mind today's TV chefs. Soon after World War Two, electricity and gas boards throughout the country decided that holding free, public cookery demonstrations was a good way to publicise and sell their appliances. Most power boards built raked theatres. Entrance was free and the public came and watched. This was a great novelty and was very popular. Regulars came earlier and earlier in order to get front-row seats. I was known as a Home Service Adviser. The job involved not only demonstrating cookery on the various cookers but giving advice and following up with home visits to any customer with difficulties.

Of the many home visits which I made, I remember going to the house of Mr. Popov, a priest of the Russian Orthodox church. Living in a very poor area of Manchester he was of a different stamp from his neighbours. Many houses had been bombed and then refurbished. Some of the tenants had not then come to grips with the unaccustomed mod. cons. In some houses, coal was stored in the bath. Mr. Popov was tall, slightly stooped and kindly. I think that he was probably wryly amused by the girl who came to give advice. His home-baked communion bread was not up to scatch and he blamed the new oven. I had to go back several times to test the cooker and indeed to bake the bread but finally concluded that his yeast recipe was to blame, not the cooker.

The job suited me down to the ground, particularly the demonstrating aspect. Any public speaking which I do nowadays seems relatively straightforward. Then, I had to produce a perfect sponge or its equivalent as well. There was no such thing as 'Here's one I made earlier.' Everything was cooked from scratch and the dish had to be finished in the given time. Subsequent public speaking has not been difficult for me. I can concentrate on speaking sense without the distraction of cooking as well. Perhaps public speaking is in the blood. My father's first post was as a lecturer with the North of Scotland College. My brother was a lawyer and he also did a great deal of public speaking in another connection. My great uncle, Rev. James Grieve was a Church of Scotland minister on North Ranaldsay. I have his Orkney chair in my Scottish cottage. The frame of these chairs is traditionally made from driftwood. The high rounded back is made from woven oat straw which also forms the wings and sometimes a hood, to exclude draughts, rather like an upturned cradle. His son defected to the Church of England via Oxford and became a canon of Carlisle Cathedral. He was the last private individual in the British Isles to be a Weather Station for the country's Meteorological Office.

I have always felt fortunate to be here at all as my death was announced before my birth. This was long before the development of high tech scans. When I gave birth myself, decades later, in West Africa, the most sophisticated prenatal device was a conical gadget like a little silver flower vase. It was placed, wide side downwards on the patient's stomach. By putting their ear to the base the doctor or nurse could hear the baby's heartbeat. Shortly before I was born, the doctor told my mother that her baby was dead. She felt sure that all was well and his gloomy prognosis was proved wrong. I was born one snowy morning. I cannot exactly claim that this somewhat negative start has made me thrive on discouragement, but perhaps at least it has made me more willing to tackle some unlikely challenges. The doctor did not fare so well as he was beheaded as a prisoner of war of the Japanese.

When I started writing about skiing, I had not written anything for publication before. My only literary effort had been to keep a daily diary since I was fourteen. Even then, publication eluded me at the most modest level. The local newspaper ran an article about a new X-ray department at the hospital which had been opened by the mayor and other dignitaries. The headline read: 'Civic Heads X-rayed.' I sent it off to Punch magazine with the caption 'And high time too.' It resulted in my first 'Editor regrets.'

My home life was privileged and comfortable. We had two cars, cleaned by a chaffeur every Sunday. Our most enthusiastic gardener was Jimmy, whose previous job had been digging graves. Flinging spades full of earth over his shoulder he was often in danger of disappearing down a rapidly deepening hole. This was an extreme interpretation of the double digging of a trench for vegetables as required by my father. He was succeeded by Joe, champion of the local bowls team. His proud boast was that he had had his 'foot in most gardens in Hale.' We soon discovered why. His pipe smoke could be spotted wreathing its way up through the trees in the orchard. Nearby would be discarded eggshells from our hens, from which he had supped a non-alcoholic eggnog. Loftily ignoring their gender, my brother had named the hens after Scottish kings; I was upset one day to discover that Alba was on my plate, or a slice of Alba anyway.

Some people consider it as self-seeking and pushy when a woman suddenly branches out in new directions. As I have made my way along my recent road the outlook of friends and acquaintances has been interesting. The young son of a well known newscaster said to my husband: 'You must sometimes think that your wife has taken leave of her senses.' I was just starting to lead a life of my own and his remark quite took my breath away. Perhaps the glass ceiling still exists even in young minds and older women are not expected to stray far from hearth and home.

True friends ask about my progress and appear interested in my achievements, in the same way as I am enthusiastically interested in theirs. Some acquaintances adopt a slightly disapproving stance, almost as though I have done something not entirely creditable. It's a poor heart that never rejoices. Others choose to ignore my new role altogether and try to push me firmly back into the 'little woman' mould. Like most women at that time, I had until then existed as an adjunct of others. I began as a daughter and a sister. I became a fiancée and then a wife. After that I was a mother. Although I never had any fault to find with this system of identification, it was still exhilarating unexpectedly to become myself, in my own right.

Life as a mother has never been dull, though. One day, I went to my son's school in order to help to sew some costumes for the school play. I was put to work in a little laundry room, complete with ancient sewing machine. At one point the door opened and a maid came in. She looked at me and said 'Fancy you being Rowley's mother!' She said it several times in a marvelling sort of way. I never discovered whether I was worse or better than she expected.

When a woman, particularly an older one, travels alone, there is often comment and pity for the spouse left at home. But it is essential to be alone, to be flexible, to make plans, change them and to go off at unforeseen tangents in order to produce original and interesting copy. Travel writing is, after all, work, albeit in its most pleasant form. What is satisfying is that criticism does not matter as my life has become so interesting. Nothing can detract from that: I make up my own mind where I go and what arrangements to make. When men travel abroad on business they usually go alone and nobody expects anything different. On their return they are semi-heroes.

Most lives are divided into phases by time and circumstances. Had I thought about it at all, I suppose that I would have naively imagined that my life would follow the pattern of my early years, secure in those long gone prewar childhood days. I had travelled with my parents and marriage took me to West Africa. But it was not until I started to travel independently for work that I made any major decisions.

Although nobody could have guessed it at the time when I first skied, the wheels had then started to roll to take me to new horizons. Life is mostly timing, often wrong. But sometimes the tumblers fall into place and things work out amazingly. That is what happened to me.

A chance meeting in an Austrian restaurant introduced me to the editors of a ski magazine. They were intrigued that I had just begun to ski at fifty-one. There is nothing particularly amazing about that but they seemed to think that there was. I was delighted to meet them and we had a merry meal together. When I got home I wrote an article about starting to ski late and they published it. Knowing now how difficult it can be to place articles, this was a lucky break. The day when the magazine arrived was tremendously exciting. Instead of paying me for my first ever article the magazine sent me alone on a press trip to Yugoslavia. My late flowering career as a ski writer was thus launched.

Ideas crowded into my head. As most destinations had already been written about I had to find unusual ski spots which might appeal to editors. This led me to the world's most unlikely places, including Antarctica, the High Atlas and the Andes. Eventually I expanded my field to include unusual pursuits apart from skiing. There was a huge element of chance in the whole business and I was immensely curious to see just how far my newfound career could be pursued.

The press trip to Yugoslavia was a great success. It was quite a contrast to life as it had been before. I was sent out as a travel writer and was met at Ljubljana airport by a guide. He was a dare devil driver and we sped along icy roads from one ski resort to the next almost on two wheels. I skied every slope around Sarejevo and rounded it all off by going down the Olympic bobsleigh run. Although the original bob sleigh had been replaced by a sort of plastic bath tub, it was still hair-raising. I sat in the middle with a helmet on and screamed most of the way down. The magazine published that article too.

When I was in Sarejevo, the tourist board lost no time in showing me other leisure attractions. The most striking was a video of tourists on wooden rafts floating down a river complete with rapids. This was the river Tara, marking the boundary between Bosnia-Herzegovina and Montenegro. The country was just beginning to find its feet in the tourism market. It had been held together by a fragile thread for some time after Tito's death. Tragically, before too long, all this was changed by the break-up of Yugoslavia.

Events in my life began to move fast. Aiming for the best, I rang the travel editor of the Daily Telegraph. She accepted my proposal for an article on river rafting. It was a gem of a commission as it opened all sorts of doors.

I kept her letter of confirmation, addressed to Miss Rowlerson. I have always been amused at this aspect of being an older writer; people are inclined to assume that the person they are meeting at the airport will be a young lissome nineteen year old. What a let down when I stagger into Arrivals with my lived-in face. It has its advantages too, of course. Travelling with a group, all usually younger, I look as though I know what I am doing even if this is not the case

Soon I was off on the rafting expedition. In Dubrovnik for a few days I was shown all the sights. Then the big day came. I boarded a bus for the town of Foca which was subsequently blasted to pieces in the ensuing conflict. The bus had an alarming crack in the windscreen but nobody seemed bothered about it so I sat back and went with the flow. Foca was a pretty little town which had several mosques with tall graceful spires. The hotel was another story. In my room, the sheets looked as though they had not been changed, there was only a thin dribble of water from the shower and the rest of the plumbing was uninviting. But none of this mattered as next day I joined a busload of holiday makers which took us to the head of the Tara river.

In times past, pine trees were cut down from the surrounding forests and then floated down the river to a furniture factory. Then it was decided to lash the logs together to make crude rafts which would take tourists. The logs were roughly twenty feet long and several joined together made a raft about eight feet wide. The journey took three days and was popular.

With a drop in altitude of sixteen hundred feet from the boarding point to our destination, there were several stretches of rapids, their ferocity depending upon recent rains. Water proof clothing would be provided if required.

After a two hours' drive from Foca, we crossed the river's only bridge and gasped as we looked down to the waters far below. Eventually we reached the point where the rudimentary rafts were waiting. We were to travel in a convoy of six. We were each allowed to take just one small holdall. I made sure that mine was waterproof as it would be stored with all the others on the raft. Everything else which I had brought with me was left in a suitcase in Foca. At night we would be sleeping ashore on sun loungers in tents, two to a tent. I gained by being a journalist as I had a tent to myself each night. As well as the minimum change of clothes, I took a pillowcase. With my day clothes folded inside, it made a good pillow.

There were a dozen or so people on each raft. Provisions were carried in a hot-box which contained our lunch and other necessities for the day. These were wrapped in a tarpaulin. Between the logs, keeping cool, floated bottles of water and Loza, a single distilled Slivovic plum brandy. A crate of beer was lashed to the side. Steering was by means of a large rough wooden paddle, the manipulation of which was made easier by putting a pad of fresh leaves between it and the logs each day.

Most of my shipmates were teenagers on school holidays. Our raftsmen, known as splavars, were a father and son team. Their word was Law.

As we set off it was sultry and overcast. I was glad to be wearing waterproofs. Midgies danced but were not too much of a problem. With a loud, pseudo Red Indian cry from Adam, the father, we were off. The skies cleared. The water was so low that soon we went aground on some rocks. Jaimo, the son, clambered overboard in his thigh-high waders and prised us free with his axe. His girl friend announced that she had a sore throat and swigged deeply from the communal brandy bottle.

We arrived at the first night stop, our legs a bit shaky even after such a short time afloat. Having found the tents and settled ourselves, it was time to eat. The camp warden had already put a whole sheep on a spit over an open fire-pit to cook. Its eyes had turned white and looked at me unflinchingly. This put an end to any of my ideas of tucking in. But never had the alternative of dry bread and runny honey tasted so good. It was washed down with coffee and I was surprised as ever to see how quickly water boils over an open fire.

From sheer exhaustion and plenty of fresh air I slept like a top despite the rather uncomfortable conditions. I had the impression that the splavars hardly slept at all as there was singing for most of the night. The first time that I saw Adam in the morning, he was sitting at the river bank being shaved by a minion.

A gloriously clear morning brought water so low at one point that the men and boys got out, waded ashore and scrambled along the rocks at the riverside in order to reduce the weight of the laden raft There was much splashing and macho shouting from the young bloods, eager to impress the girls. Despite the warm sun, the water was icy cold, fed with snow-melt from the distant hills. One of the teenagers from Ljubljana produced a guitar which he strummed, so we drifted along to music. At times our progress was so slow that we were overtaken by butterflies. Drifting in the current, little bubbles kept pace with us. It was a truly tranquil scene.

The second night was much like the first. But on the next day, we met turbulence with real white water rapids. But we were soon in calmer waters again. Adam pointed out where he had been with the Partisans in 1943, up in the woods. There was temporary panic when the beer crate almost broke loose, great roars of laughter about losing our bottle. This led to horse play with the people on the raft behind and they decided to overtake us. Their wizened splavar drove his axe quite dangerously into the back of our raft. But we managed to break away to shouts of triumph.

A hunter on the bank appeared from nowhere and jumped aboard. He was wearing a loden jacket and a gold watch. He offered me a cognac bottle and binoculars, in that order. It was a bit early for the former. He had apparently been expecting to have a lift from us. A factory owner, he had been fishing for salmon trout. He told us that he had seen a bear on his last visit.

There was no other river traffic. My journey ended at seven that evening. The others would continue as far as the factory in Vizebad. I have often wondered what happened to the affable teenagers in all the subsequent trouble. Most of them would have been of military age by the time that Yugoslavia finally fell apart.

I went back to the same hotel which I had found so dreadful a few days before. I was shown up to the same room and I thought that I had landed in heaven. The bed had sheets on it, whether they had been changed or not no longer seemed important. I was grateful for the little drip of water from the shower and there was a loo.

I began to be asked on other press trips. One of these, unrelated to skiing, was to Sicily. As we flew in, I looked down into the great red maw of Mount Etna and was surprised to hear that enough snow falls there in the winter months for there to be skiing.

The flight home was amusing. Travelling as a group of journalists, we were asked in turns to go up to the cockpit. It was a myriad of dials plus dozens of knobs. Over the radio, a new route was suggested, cutting off a corner near Genoa. One of the pilots said that he had recently seen the Northern Lights over Europe but they eluded us on this occasion. We had already passed Elba and Nice was behind. When I read my notes at home later, I wondered 'What on earth does that mean: "Nice behind"?

There was radar sweep beyond each of the two pilots in the BAC 111. The scale could be altered easily. The pilot, Reg, was flying the plane buttering the roll of his lap supper at the same time. I fleetingly wondered if I was going to relive that episode in the Canadian film where both pilots collapse from food poisoning, leaving me to be talked down. I could see myself breathing a great sigh of relief as, on landing, I thanked the crew of the hastily summoned fire engine. In fact pilots still eat different food on the flight as well as allowing eight hours from 'bottle to throttle.'

On my way back to rejoin a fellow writer, I saw two Sicilians playing cards with a strange pack. I had seen these Napoletane cards and had bought some so I was anxious to see how the game was played. I sat with them for a little while. They were brothers, hairdressers, one with a salon in Milton Keynes, the other in the 'Art of 'Ammersmith' as he put it. They offered to trim my wild hair there and then but we decided that it would make too much mess.

I eventually returned to my place. The journalist in the next seat had not seen my encounter with the card players. When she asked how I had got on, meaning in the cockpit, I replied: 'Oh, fine, they're a couple of Sicilian hairdressers.' No wonder she went a bit pale.

On my return, I again rang the travel editor of the Telegraph and she agreed to take a piece from me on skiing Mount Etna. Off I went to Taormina for the second time, in February. I could see that the volcano was wearing a cape of snow. This boded well. But I was dismayed when I looked out next morning to see that the snow appeared to have gone. But I was assured that it was still there. It had been covered in the night by lava dust blowing from the ever-smoking cone. Skiing is on a multi-layered sandwich of snow and lava dust. The hot dust crystallises the snow, making it rather granular.

Etna has roughly two hundred peaks but only about nine craters are active. The ski area, since destroyed by devastating eruptions, was a long way from any danger.

On the drive up the winding lava-block paved road, white violets bloomed in the scant shelter of snow covered rocks. The driver was a city man wearing white socks and black pointed shoes. When we reached the snows, he stepped out of the car and picked his way daintily through the strange substance. His name, Orazio, was no doubt a corruption of Nelson's first name. The sailor watered his fleet at the spring of Arethusa off Syracuse. The spring there yields a hundred gallons of fresh water a second. Nelson, on his way to battle with Napoleon, felt that victory was assured. Thereafter there has always been a ship in the Royal Navy named Arethusa. Also in gratitude, Nelson assumed the title Duke of Bronte after the nearby Sicilian town.

It was a misty day but an old drag lift, imported from mainland Italy, pulled me up the slope and the skiing was fine. It made a great article for the Daily Telegraph.

Early on I realised that once you have mentioned any future goals to anyone, you must carry them out. It is no good being like the man who is going to give up smoking tomorrow. People soon lose interest and you lose your momentum. Conversely, it is a good idea not to share plans with too many people as somebody may easily climb onto your bandwagon of ideas.

The importance of acting on ideas was brought home to me when I told a colleague on the Bench that I intended to go to Alaska. When we met again, quite a long time afterwards, she asked me how I had got on. To my shame, I had to admit that I had not been there. After our conversation, I put things right immediately and luckily found an outlet for an article. Since then I have visited and written about that intriguing wilderness many times.

'My Journey Home from Canada, 1943'

Norma Grieve, Hale, Cheshire.

I had been living in Canada for two years and nine months when news came that passages had been booked for my brother, Valentine, and me to come home by way of Portugal. This is an account of our trip home:

Val and I left Toronto on January 29th, after being vaccinated against Smallpox. We took a 'Sleeper' to New York where we arrived after an uneventful night's sleep. In point of fact, I was awakened by a queer 'jiggling' of my mattress. I poked my head out of the cubicle curtains to see the chocolate-coloured face of the porter. In a deep, resonant voice, he said 'Noo Yoak.' After alighting from the train, we took a taxi to 'Hotel Bristol.' I should like to draw attention to the colour of the taxis. I think I can truthfully say that there is not a taxi in New York which is painted a sombre colour. Scarlet, sky-blue, yellow and green... these are the order of the day. Our taxi was a modest yellow with splashes of black.

A homely primrose would have blushed at the colour. We were given the keys to our rooms and we went there to find that we had been given two very nice ones. After having a wash and our breakfast (which consisted of two thin eggs which were cracked and put in a glass container, toast and coffee) we took a taxi to Thomas Cook's office to collect some money. Having completed that trip, we proceeded to the Portuguese Consul's office,where we were to collect our Portuguese Visas. After standing in a queue at that place for about half an hour we at last reached the head of the queue where were stated our needs. The girl looked through the files, but she could not find our Visas. Val and I then waited for another half hour while the girl phoned to another office to find out if they knew anything about it there. After a very anxious wait, we were very much relieved to hear that our Visa was all right after all.

We spent the rest of the day looking in the shop windows. Incidentally, I bought a hat which, since I arrived home, has many times been described as a mushroom which should have been picked a week ago (not very complimentary to the New York fashions.)

In all we spent a week in New York, during which time we went to several movies and went over the NBC studios with a very kind friend. During this tour I was 'Telivised' (sic). This was very interesting. The only unpleasant part was the very bright glare of the lamps.

On the 3rd of February, we went by train to Philadelphia, and I would like to add that I left New York with a temperature of 103o. On reaching Philadelphia, we took a taxi to the docks. This taxi was painted dark blue, and was driven by a woman.

We went through the Customs office,and there all our printed matter was taken away, to be returned that night on the ship. (Footnote: Even at that age, my brother was a very keen chess player and a lot of this took the form of correspondence chess. He had with him a lot of postcards from various opponents, all written in the chess 'shorthand' which is still used today. The customs men were not familiar with it and it aroused suspicion. Fortunately they found someone who was able to confirm its innocence.) We then went aboard the vessel, which was a Portuguese one. On the bow, in shining letters, 'Serpa Pinto, Lisboa.' Our cabins were on the top deck with an open deck running along the outside.

About two o'clock, I was awakened with a terrific noise which was going on outside. I looked out of the porthole and saw to my surprise that the dock men were loading cargo and were on a night shift. This kept me awake until five o'clock when they had completed their shift and gone home to bed.

That day was spent in watching the cargo being loaded. The cargo was Red Cross boxes for our prisoners of war.

February 5th was also spent in the same manner.

On the 6th, we set sail for Bermuda. We were held up in the river that night, due to a very heavy fog. On the 7th we sailed again, and the weather started to get uncomfortably rough. The storm was very bad on the 8th, and the ship suffered severe losses in the china line. The next day, we sighted Bermuda through the storm.

On Wednesday February 10th, we sighted Bermuda through calm waters, and made for those islands.

I shall never forget my first sight of that tropical Paradise.

Bermuda stands out in my mind as a landscape of green grass dotted with beautiful blossoms, white-roofed houses, and a deep blue sea. As we went through the narrow straits which were the gate-way to Bermuda we were met by a battleship which shepherded us into port. The inland sea was full of lovely little islands which looked delightful against the blue of the sea.

After a lot of 'Palaver' we were at last allowed ashore. There we walked around the small township of Hamilton.

Bermuda is often called the Millionaires' Playground and this name is very well suited to Bermuda. Everything sold in Hamilton is twice or three times the amount that it is in Canada.

We did not sail again until 11th so we all had a very enjoyable day, staying ashore very late.

Thursday was a beautiful day on which to sail, as the weather was so marvellous.

For the next week we sailed on through tropical seas, thoroughly enjoying the warm sunshine after the freezing cold winter in Canada. During that week we were kept busy by some very interesting events. On board were 100 men from the Humphrey's Company, going out to West Africa. They arranged sports for the older children, and 'Grownups', and sports for the younger children.

Every adult on the boat was asked to contribute 5s. towards the prizes, and then the races were held up and down the deck.I was very relieved when I won 2/6 for the women's obstacle race. Before the race I was in a state of bankruptcy. On Thursday 18th, we sighted The Azores which are a group of islands just two days off Lisbon.

Before I go on with the trip, I should like to go back to a very important fact which I had forgotten. On mentioning that the boat was a Portuguese one, I did not say that only about five of the whole crew could speak English. Our steward could not, so we could never get anything brought to the cabin. If the steward had spoken French, it would not have been much good, as Val's French and mine are terribly shaky.

On reaching the Azores, we were told that we would not be allowed ashore, as we would only be staying for a few hours.

The merchants came out in their little boats, and set up pulleys by the side of the ship. We sent down coins, and they sent up baskets full of fruit.

We set sail again, and on the night of 19th, a fancy dress ball was arranged. We had a lot of fun that night, and we did not go to bed until about two o'clock the next morning. Now, as it happens, the 20th is my birthday, and we sighted land during the ball. We all went to bed very excited and I was awakened by the steward putting his head around the door, and saying 'Lisboa..' We landed that day and went to the Parque Palacio Hotel. This hotel had been built so recently, that hot-waterpipes had not yet been installed! The food was perfectly foul and one time we had cat. I know it was cat for a fact, because one boy got the teeth. It is rather difficult to sum up the next month as nothing really happened, except we were given three false alarms about coming home.

When we finally went, we were aroused about five o'clock in the morning by a very drowsy night porter who knocked frantically on our doors thinking, I suppose, that we were never going to wake up. We gathered our luggage (44lbs. maximum) and made our way to the British Overseas Airways Office, walking down the main street,singing 'There'll Always Be an England.' When we arrived at the office, we were given coffee to drink. Having ourselves previously been weighed-in, our luggage was weighed, and we sat down to wait for the bus which was to take us to the airport at Cintra.

On reaching that place, we were given more coffee, and then we went through the customs officials, to see that we were not taking too much fruit out of the country.

The plane upon which we were to go was a Douglas DC2. We boarded that vehicle, and sat down in very comfortable seats to wait for it to take off.

We were on a Dutch plane, with a Dutch crew, and they are meant to be very efficient, so we did not feel in the least (apprehensive?) of the six hours plane trip ahead of us.

We took off at 8.32, and the take-off was very smooth. If one were deaf and blind, one would not have known that we were taking off. We leant back, and fastened our safety belts. After we were up in the air, we rose and rose until, when asking how high up we were, I was informed that we were up 11,000 feet. After a while, my ears began to ache, but with chewing gum, this soon went away.

About 11.30, we had lunch. This consisted of:

1 leg of chicken
3 slices of ham
Salad with: lettuce, tomatoes, ½ egg each, beetroot, cucumber, and green pepper,
a piece of fruit cake
an orange
a banana
two rolls cheese,
butter
cheese biscuits
coffee,
Chicklets chewing gum.

This was all wrapped up in grease-proof paper and tasted very fresh. We were also supplied with chewing gum.

You might be interested to hear that Baron Rothchild was on our plane and he told me that he had just escaped from France, and he had walked from France to Spain, and it took him eight days to do so.

Looking down, we saw tiny cloudlets and below it the blue of the Atlantic Ocean. As I mentioned previously, we were flying at a height of 11,000 feet, the clouds looked just like fluffy fragments of cotton wool, spread out upon an azure background.

About 1.30, one of the crew came along, and locked pieces of blackout wood over the windows. He said that the landing regulations made this compulsory, as the passengers were not meant to see the coastal defences.

About a quarter past two, we started to lose height, and we were supplied with ammonia capsules, which one is meant to smell if one feels at all faint during the landing. As it happens, I felt all right except for a piercing pain in my ears.

As we neared the airport, we heard fighter planes coming up to meet us. You see, we had to be recognised as a friendly aircraft before we could land. The drone of the engines was deafening as they flew nearer to look at our markings.

As we descended, we hit air pocket after air pocket until we finally touched England's soil after three years' absence from that country.

During the flight, we were given health forms to fill in along with our landing cards, stating if we had any infectious diseases during the past two weeks. After handing these into the airport doctor at the south country airport, we proceeded to the customs office.

There we were asked to declare how much money we were bringing into England. Val and I went just before Baron Rothchild. When asked how much we had, we informed them that we were bringing in the enormous sum of 2/6d. When questioned, Baron Rothchild put his hand into his pocket, and pulled out a wad of notes, at least five inches high. The poor customs official nearly went into a swoon when he saw all the money which the baron calmly produced. After that little incident, we were taken to the baggage department, where our luggage was examined.

Of all the rotten jobs in war-time, I think that the baggage inspector is one of the men to be pitied most. He has baskets full of fruit and lets people take them home with them when he has just about forgotten the taste of orange, the banana or the pineapple. It is not so bad not having fruit, if it isn't passing under your nose continually, but in the case of the customs man, I think that it is very hard lines. I felt so sorry for the man who went over our luggage that I gave him a rather hot and soggy orange. He seemed very pleased to have it all the same. After being given a cup of tea, Val and I were taken in an RAF car to the station. We caught the Manchester train at five past five and sat down to await our arrival at Crewe where we were to change for Alderley Edge.

On arriving at that station in the black-out, Val stepped out of the train before it had stopped and fell headlong on the platform. I of course could not do anything because the train was still going quite fast. Val got up in a stew and ran so hard that he overtook the carriage in which I was standing and reached the engine... I might have mentioned before that we had exactly 10 minutes to change trains. As soon as I could alight, I dived up to the engine and got Val, then we dived back again to the luggage, pulled it out and then dived off to the train for Alderley Edge.

We employed a girl porter to help with our luggage and on arriving at the train we informed her that we were 'broke' and scrambled into the carriage.

We arrived at Alderley Edge to find Mum and Dad waiting for us. It turned out that they did not know that we were in the UK until we were actually on the train, when a friend at the aerodrome phoned them to say that we were on the train.

That is the end of the narrative. I hope that it has brought a little interest to you as I have tried to state the events just as they took place.

'... dazed and sooty...'

Chapter Two

(All names with a legal connection have been changed.)

*When I am old and grey and full of sleep
I won't have to bother counting sheep.*

The second unexpected lurch in life-at the age of fifty-one-was being called for jury service. I still have the letter. It changed my life. Jurors are selected at random from the electoral roll. Some people dread jury service and regard it as an imposition. I viewed my letter as a stroke of luck. The first time that I walked into the court, I wondered what I had been doing with my life. The whole judicial process was fascinating and impressive. The courthouse was an old stone building, dating back several centuries. The courtroom where we sat was virtually unchanged from its early days. Stained glass skylights shed a garish glow. The dock, with cell access, was surrounded by fearsome iron spikes. It was a chastening thought that, in the past, people stood there with their lives in the balance. When the death penalty was in force, executions took place in the nearby prison.

In the first case on which I was a juror the charge was burglary. The accused was an antique dealer. He and his co-defendant were charged with stealing silver and jewellery from a large country house. The evidence was damning.

Mr. Clacket, the defendant in question, was caught standing in the garden, his presumed partner in crime just emerging from a window above, bag of loot in hand. The allegation was that the bag was about to be thrown to Mr. Clacket below. 'Things are not always as they seem,' said the young barrister for the defence. He was instantly recognisable, the son of one of our best known actors. Like his father, he was dark and good looking so this added zest to the proceedings. His first act, getting to his feet, had not been trouble-free: the barrister for the prosecution was sitting on the tail of his gown. In fact, his first words to the court were: 'If my learned friend will allow me to rise.'

He turned to the jury and said 'Ladies & Gentlemen of the jury, when I was a small boy, eight or nine years old, I was walking one day with my friend, near to a railway line. To my horror my friend suddenly leapt over the fence, ran down onto the line, grabbed the handle which controlled the points and moved it. I was appalled. Imagine the danger had a train come hurtling along at that moment, diverted onto the wrong rail. It could have sped on and hit a train coming in the opposite direction. So, Ladies & Gentlemen of the jury (for an unkind moment I imagined that this speech had been well rehearsed in front of the mirror) I told my friend that he must move the points back to their original position. The handle was very stiff, he could not move it. Without hesitation I also jumped the fence and ran down onto the track. I put my hands over his and we pushed together and managed to put the points back to their original position. Had a passerby come along at that moment he would have fairly assumed that I was as guilty as my friend of interfering with the points.

This is precisely what happened in the case of Mr. Clacket. Hearing that his friend intended to commit a burglary, he raced to the house, arriving just as his friend was emerging from the window with the spoils of his crime. When Mr. Clacket was spotted he was in fact pleading with his friend to leave the stolen goods behind.

So you see, Ladies & Gentlemen of the jury, things are not always as they seem.'

In his summing up, the judge's opening sentence was: 'I am not going to indulge in any boyhood reminiscences.'

Earlier on we had been told to appoint a foreman. I was at that point in the washroom and emerged to hear who had been selected.

When I related all the details to a friend, she said 'Why don't you become a magistrate?' If being picked for jury service is a matter of luck, becoming a magistrate is up to you. Shortly before that period, suitable candidates would have been 'approached' by existing 'beaks' but things had recently become more democratic. Before a year had elapsed, I had been appointed a magistrate, a Justice of the Peace. The experience gave me completely new insights into human nature and I found the whole justice system gripping. Even lay members, on this, the lowest rung of the judicial ladder, have great powers.

It had taken some years after my return from West Africa for all of this to happen. One reason that I had been leading a fairly quiet conventional life was that my health and energies had been seriously depleted by fifteen years in the tropics. Repeated bouts of malaria and also dengue fever had taken their toll. It was a long time after my return before I really felt fighting fit and raring to go. I have never been a hot weather creature and the African climate was a trial to me. I returned to the UK periodically, having lost a deal of weight; my father would remark that I was 'all eyes and teeth.' With a hard frost and a foot of snow, I am in my natural element. So it all came together at the right time.

Having embarked up on two new careers, the Law and journalism, I never looked back. It all seemed a perfectly natural progression and it was so lucky to slip effortlessly into both worlds. Thus I came to lead a life of my own.

Prison sentences are not as frequent from magistrates' courts as the press would lead one to believe. The first time when sitting on the Bench we sent somebody to prison was chastening. The chair was taken by a quiet, unassuming colleague. He worked as an engineer for the telephone company and had a moment of angst when he arrived that day. He thought that he had left his reading glasses in somebody's guttering. After sentencing the man to a prison term, we went into the retiring room. He said to me: 'I don't enjoy sending people to prison but I do it so that those who would enjoy it don't do it.' Wise words. Hopefully those who might enjoy the power are weeded out during the selection process. When I first started, I felt that there but for luck went I and I wanted to let everyone off. Although one hopes not to grow a thick skin, one's judgment soon becomes more realistic.

At its inception in 1361 by Edward 111 the principle of the Criminal Justice system was that one should be tried by one's peers. Possibly up to a hundred years before that there had been peacekeepers. With isolated communities and limited travel, this meant that defendants would be known to the local Justice of the Peace. Over the centuries, the system has evolved whereby the defendant is usually a stranger. This does not apply worldwide. On remote Norfolk Island, off Australia, any defendant is usually known to all the inhabitants.

Many cases are fairly straightforward. Most criminal cases come first to magistrates who, unpaid, deal with 98%. Even the most mundane I found interesting; there would always be a human twist. One man caused an accident because, he said, not only was the sun in his eyes but his eyes were full of tears after a break-up with his girl friend.

During other hearings, some extraordinary defences were put forward. There was a particular lawyer in the town who seemed to specialise in unlikely defences. My heart would drop if I saw him heading for the courts.

One case was of a man who was passing the house of his wife who had recently divorced him. He was accused of kicking in the glass panel of the front door. The prosecution outlined the case, telling us that the former wife was looking out of her bedroom window one day. Her previous husband was passing by. (I had learnt that, in court, no former spouse was referred to as an 'Ex.' It was always 'former' husband/wife or 'previous.' Similarly, the term 'Vice' was not used in connection with any Bench office, 'Deputy' being deemed more fitting.) Her previous husband looked up and saw his former wife at the window. It was alleged that he began swearing at her. He then flung open the gate, ran down the steps and kicked in the glass panel. What could have been more open and shut ?

Trust Mr. Morton to come to the accused's assistance with a vengeance. True to form, again he had an amazing explanation. According to him, the defendant was strolling along in the sunshine one day. He happened to pass the house where he had lived with his former wife. Looking up, he saw her at the bedroom window. He called out a pleasant greeting to her and they passed the time of day very amicably. Unfortunately, as he leant on the gate, the catch gave way and the gate flew open. The man was hurled forward, not falling down the steps as one might have expected. No, it was nothing as predictable as that. According to his wizard of an advocate, he landed on a disused pram. With his legs sticking out in front, he hurtled down the steps at great speed and his feet inadvertently went through the glass door panel. It is sometimes difficult to keep a judicially straight face. Those words 'landed on a disused pram' never fail to lift my mood.

Magistrates sit with judges on Appeals. Lunching with a judge was often an amusing business. On one occasion, there was a case in the Crown court which necessitated extra security. Unbeknown to the judge, the police had visited his house earlier that day and had placed sensitive security pads under a rug at the front door. His wife was out and had not had time to warn him. Arriving home, he decided to lay and light a fire in the drawing room and donned an apron. Having done this, he looked through the window and saw two plump pigeons sitting in the drive. Thinking that they would make a tasty supper, he picked up his gun, went outside and shot them. At that moment, having been alerted by the pressure pad, two cars bristling with policemen came roaring up his drive. The judge told me that they were surprised to see him standing outside, wearing an apron and with a smoking shotgun in his hands.

We had our regulars. On this particular day, we had not seen Mr. Barker for a while. At one time, he had popped into the dock quite regularly, answering various charges, anything from driving without insurance to abstracting electricity without payment. His colourful, somewhat grimy self had brightened up many an otherwise routine sitting. Indeed, his appearance got more and more unkempt as the years went by, due, no doubt, to the fact that he doubled as a part time chimney sweep. Often he looked as if he had just survived some kind of explosion, emerging dazed and sooty from the scene of a catastrophe. His illegal use of electricity culminated in the local power company's cutting off his supply by dint of digging a large hole in the road outside his house.

But on this day he appeared scrubbed and self-assured. As he entered the dock he removed a large brown floppy corduroy cap which he wore at a jaunty angle. He did seem to be limping, though. He told us, to our surprise, that until last month he had been a factory supervisor. He explained that he had received 'quite a lot of court thingeys lately' and said that these had left him 'all over the place.' In his spare time, he was repairing an Austin Allegro for a girl owner who had asked him 'to do up' her car. He assumed that there was a current test certificate. When he took the car out on a test run, he had unfortunately assumed incorrectly and now pleaded guilty to the offence of driving a vehicle with no test certificate. His fine new career had come to an abrupt end when an injury to his leg forced him to stop work. His fearsome limp proved this.

It was appropriate to fine him for the offence. I asked him about his income. He said that he was now receiving benefit from the state. When I asked him to tell us what sort of benefit it was, he answered that he was receiving Infidelity Benefit. (It was of course Incapacity Benefit.)With commendable perception, one glance at our startled faces made him realise that this was not quite right. He swiftly corrected himself and said that he was receiving Infertility Benefit. He never got it right. Replacing his outsize cap, he limped out of court, blissfully unaware that he had credited the government with a whole new range of benefits.

The next defendant was a fisherman from an adjoining county who was charged with having twenty-eight undersized Dover soles. Legally, only fish over a certain size may be taken from the sea. Four months previously, fisheries officials, carrying a special measure, had boarded his boat. The measure was produced in court. The defence case was that the measure was old and worn, thus causing fish to appear shorter than they were. We agreed and acquitted the man. The offending fish had been kept refrigerated in a large white polystyrene lidded box for the ensuing months and were brought to court and had thawed out on that hot summer's day. Just to ensure that the efforts to keep them had not been wasted, to the surprise of the defence I asked for the box to be opened. The resultant whiff of rotting fish speeded up proceedings. The court emptied swiftly.

One day, we were asked to issue a residence order. A mother was making the application; she had a profoundly handicapped child who needed her full attention. She also had three older children. She had never married and all the children had different fathers. Her mother had been a pub landlady. Until recently the other three children had been looked after by their grandmother but she had died a month before.

The mother was now applying for the order so that her brother could take over the care of the trio. We were told that he been convicted of committing a violent crime some years earlier but that the Social Services had no objection to his assuming responsibility for the children. The uncle had a one bedroom flat. If the residence order were granted, his progress up the housing list would be accelerated and the children would thus have a more suitable home. He would also have the authority to have them admitted to hospital in any emergency.

We retired to read the prepared reports. To our surprise, we saw that the violent crime referred to had been one of murder for which he had served a period of imprisonment.

When we returned to court, the sister and her murderer brother were still sitting side by side and a more wholesome pair you never saw. When we asked for an elaboration on the violent crime, the social worker dismissed it quite lightly by explaining that it had been 'basically, just a normal murder, really.' There was no better solution to the family problem and we granted the order.

In the Crown Court soon after, I sat on appeals with another judge who had a knack of terrifying new, inexperienced barristers. One, pleading for his client not to be sent to prison, said, 'As you know, Your Honour, some defendants come out of prison better than they go in.' Judge: 'You've got it the wrong way round.' Another advocate, seeming to lose all power of logical thought, asked his client if the defendant had been asleep before he woke him up. Judge: 'It's implicit in the question.'

In another case, the defendant's mother had travelled a long way in order to speak for her son. The door opened and she was called. In limped an elderly, fluffy woman of diminutive stature. If casting a TV drama, the director would have rejected her on the grounds that she was too much of a stereotype to be believable. With a lurching gait, the woman came to the front of the court. A chair was hastily brought but she stood again for the Oath. She looked bewildered by the whole setting. The well-fed, well-groomed barrister for the Crown began to question her. Not only could she not hear him, she could not locate him either. In desperation he called out to her: 'I'm over here, Mrs. Bloggs.'

Zaria

Chapter Three

To Africa's coral strand.

Having worked for three years, marriage entailed going to live in West Africa. I had enjoyed those years of an innovative career, but at the time a wife's career usually took second place to her husband's. My contemporaries generally gave up their jobs. I had no choice as I was going abroad. In those days, it seemed a tremendous adventure, much more interesting than my friends' lives in various places in the UK.

I had yet another parting from my parents, this time at Heathrow. My brother gave me reading matter for the journey, Monica Dickens' 'No More Meadows.' It made apt reading for the trip except that the author went off to join her husband in the USA. Where I was headed was quite a different kettle of fish.

The flight in the BOAC Argonaut to Kano in Northern Nigeria soon cheered me up. The thing about flying that always delights me is that, no matter what conditions are

41

on the ground, within moments of take-off you are up in the sunshine. This reminds me of the trainee pilot who was asked to give his height and position. He said: 'I'm five foot seven and I'm sitting at the front of the aircraft.'

As on many subsequent flights, we stopped to refuel in Tripoli. Before we were allowed to leave the 'plane a man would come down the aisle and spray us with liberal amounts of the insecticide Flit. This presumably was to ensure that we were not bringing any dangerous bugs from England to Africa. After the spraying, we were then herded into an old aircraft hangar which still had bullet holes in its corrugated-iron walls, a legacy of World War Two. The six-hour night leg of the trip over the Sahara was exciting, the lights of fires winking far below. At dusk, during my early days in Africa, I often would say that there was a smell of burning. My husband would point out 'They are lighting fires all over Africa.'

Then came dawn over the desert, a lurid, violent affair and we landed at five in the morning in Kano.

Populated mainly by Muslim Hausas, the north of Nigeria has no sea access for exporting its produce or for importing essentials. Boundaries had been set many years before by the British. This geographical fact had always led to dissatisfaction from the Hausas and did not help the eventual civil disturbances which led to the so-called Biafra war in 1967. By a quirk of fate, the first and the last place where I lived in Africa was Zaria, about six hundred miles inland. Arriving in the week of the Coronation in 1953, I witnessed the whole turn of the circle from colonial rule, independence and on to anarchy and slaughter.

My husband of six months was already in Zaria. He was a produce manager for a trading company which was Unilever's largest subsidiary. At that time the company were licensed buying agents of produce for the Nigerian government. The local crops were groundnuts, cotton, Niger gum, sheanuts and chillies. Perhaps because of the fierce heat and little rain, the chillies from nearby Funtua were world-renowned and were prominently featured in Fortnum and Mason's green-grocery department. An attractive sight, on approaching a bush village at sunset, was to see the domed mud roofs shining with colour as though covered in scarlet mosaic. This effect came from red chillies being spread out to dry.

After touching down at Kano on that morning, the next part of the journey was by a West African Airways De Havilland Dove 'plane. The airline's logo was a flying elephant, which never seemed very appropriate. Not only was my luggage weighed but I was too.

Our single-storeyed house had a corrugated iron roof but it was attractive. The garage was thatched with palm fronds. As relatively cool nights followed the heat of the day, there would be loud clanging noises as the house's metal contracted. There was a large kapok tree at the back of the house. Annually, when the huge pods were ripe, they would rain down onto the roof with a noise like cannon fire. The house was built in the Lugard style, Lord Lugard having in the early days had a mandate to govern Nigeria. His influence was strong in the north.

There was a fair amount of history in the area. Not too far away was Kwatarkwashi. It was reputed to be the last place where the British army had formed a square.

According to The National Army Museum:

'The square was still in use in the 1870s, a notable occasion being at the Battle of Ulundi in 1879. One of the last major uses of the tactic was at Omdurman in 1898. The square was essentially a tactic which worked best in flat ground against badly armed colonial troops, and therefore died out in the late 19th and 20th centuries, but may have still had later, isolated uses in the right conditions.

By the time that I arrived, the massive rock outcrops at Kwatarkwashi were notorious again for sinister reasons. The caves are home to countless wild bees. A European was out in the bush there when his dog ran into a cave. Unable to persuade the dog come out, he went in to rescue it. He was bitten many times all over his body and also swallowed several hundred bees. He was found and taken some miles away to a friend's house where he died a prolonged and agonising death. The dog was never seen again.

Zaria was bizarre to me. The dusty main street was known as The Beach, rather confusing as it was so far from the sea. The name originated from the old trading days when commerce was concentrated on the coast and rivers. This was rather like the Strand in London. In trading companies, any part of West Africa was always referred to as The Coast. The Beach in Zaria was lined with various offices and primitive shops. The latter were called canteens, again from early trading days. They also had corrugated-iron roofs and were built of rough concrete blocks. They stocked mainly dry goods, sugar, flour, dried milk, tinned foods, zinc buckets, brightly enamelled plates, bales of cloth, rope and many durable items. There was no frozen food. Everything else came from the market. Our cook would set off daily and return with bones for stock making and unappetising meat, usually tough lamb. Goat, even tougher, probably slipped into the pot too, as it was cheaper. As far as I know, the most unusual meat which we ate was hartebeest, shot in the bush one day by a friend. Chickens or guinea fowl, tomatoes, onions and potatoes formed the main part of our fairly conventional diet.

Eggs had to be tested for freshness. Those which floated when put into a bucket of water had to be discarded. Guinea fowl eggs, rounder than hens' eggs, have whites which will not whip.

Like most houses, ours had cement floors which were painted with red or dark green paint. A high shine was achieved by much elbow grease and applications of appropriately coloured Cardinal Polish.

We had cast iron beds with mosquito nets which tucked in under the mattresses. On some nights, the nets would be alive with tiny fireflies, all glittering in the dark.

We took a daily anti-malarial tablet, Paludrine, which was effective for most people. I was one of the less fortunate but the disease never recurred after I came back to the UK. I contracted benign tertian malaria, rather than the more serious cerebral strain.

As a young, well-nourished European, it took all my time to keep my household running smoothly, to do what I could for our employees and to keep my family and myself in good health. I always marvelled that anything was achieved locally in view of the fierce climate, health hazards and poor medical facilities.

Zaria had mains electricity and water, though, luxuries which we would lack in other places. There was no air conditioning but there was a ceiling fan in the sitting room. The kitchen was a hovel out across the 'compound' from the back door. The cook burned unseasoned mahogany. Sawing it into small pieces was too much for him so he would push the end of quite a long branch into the fire box. As it burnt away, he would push it in further with his bare foot.

Although I always felt totally at home in Africa and never threatened in any way until my final weeks there, most things were strange and different from home. The citrus fruits, oranges, grapefruit, lemons, were all green. The only fruits which were the expected colour were limes. Apparently citrus peel turns from green to riper colours only when there is a considerable drop in night temperature.

When I first arrived, I knew little about Africa and less about the Muslim way of life. The landscape of the north and its inhabitants looked much like drawings of biblical times. Donkeys were a common means of transport, traditional dress was turbans and flowing robes. The cloth worn was mainly cotton and it was surprising, with poor washing facilities and bars of coarse soap, how white the robes looked and how clean everyone seemed to be. Muslim law requires washing before the several daily prayers, this being achieved with water poured from a kettle specifically kept for that purpose.

Necessity was certainly the mother of invention. I learnt that lesson well over the years and it has stood me in good stead. Soon after my arrival, a broken pane of glass in the house had to be replaced. The carpenter cycled up to take details. He brought no equipment with him, not even a tape measure. He went outside and returned with a piece of long grass. This he held against the window and he then bent up each end to take the size. He pocketed the grass and returned the following day with new glass which was a perfect fit.

Bicycles were status symbols. They were encased in brown paper wrapping for the journey from Europe. It was prestigious for the bicycle to appear new so the wrapping was seldom removed. If it became torn or dirty, it would be replaced. The most popular make was Raleigh and there were advertising jingles on the radio and on billboards.

One such ran:

'Raleigh for strength, Raleigh for ease,
I take my Raleigh wherever I please.'

The club, which at that time was open only to Europeans, was the Mecca of our life. Dances were held on Saturdays. The most played record, a vinyl 78rpm, was 'April in Portugal.' The range of flying and crawling creatures was certainly wide: beetles the size of dinner plates would bang about, colliding with the light bulbs. There were lots of lizards, ranging from the gecko to large purple ones with orange tails. Disconcertingly if a lizard is trapped by its tail, it can discard that appendage and carry on as usual.

On dance nights the men wore dinner jackets and the women long dresses. These were quite practical and in fact stopped our legs from getting bitten by mosquitoes. One evening there was a scream as a woman discovered a large lizard walking across her stomach, having crawled up inside her voluminous skirt.

The cinema screen was outside and made of cement. The surface became hot in the sun during the day. When the film began, we would see insects crawling all over the screen and lizards climbing up and down the heroine's face, enjoying the warmth. On one occasion, there was suddenly a great, panicky shout of 'machici.' Everyone moved very fast as a snake had slithered into the area set aside for the show. Those sitting on chairs leapt swiftly on to their seats, others fled on foot. The snake was eventually tracked down, bludgeoned to death and then the show went on. The film was Dr. Strangelove.

The telephone service was unreliable. The works were contained in a wooden box on the floor beside the phone. The battery inside had to be kept topped up with distilled water. In order to be connected to the operator, a handle was cranked and someone, with luck, would answer.

It was not too difficult to learn the rudiments of the Hausa language. The level required and attained by District Officers, who attended courses in the UK prior to arriving in the country, was above that picked up on the spot. But it was good to be able to speak to people in their own language, particularly if they did not speak English. I am always surprised that recent TV programmes on the joys of relocating to France or Spain seem to gloss over the great drawback of a language barrier. The company for which my husband worked awarded £50 to any of the Europeans who passed their Hausa exam. By 1959 this largesse was extended to the wives. I was the third wife to pass. The final paragraph of the congratulatory letter which I received from the General Manager reads: 'May I offer my sincere congratulations on your success which I am sure will be a great incentive to the wives of other members of the Management staff.' It sums up attitudes of that period.

The exam itself was oral and fairly informal. Two or three European Hausa speakers would assemble and then a Hausaman would be asked to attend. He might be a watchman or a storekeeper or just someone who was walking along the street at the time, as was the case in my exam. I was told to have a conversation with the man, asking about his job, family and so on. I discovered that he was a farmer. He said that he grew potatoes. I asked if he grew sweet potatoes or the more usual variety. He said that he grew both. I then asked him how they differed. He said that he never knew which sort would come up, the seeds were the same, it was a matter of luck, 'Sai Allah', which variety grew. A mild wrangle went on for some time, in some detail. I was completely baffled and appealed to the panel in English if I had missed or misunderstood something. But they laughed and said that that was what the farmer thought. So that was that. The panel were satisfied that my vocabulary was adequate and that I could be understood and could understand. With the fifty pounds, I bought a hand sewing machine which was soon pressed into use. Jonathan, my small energetic son, turned the handle for me with great gusto.

Not everyone learning a language in other parts of the world fared so well. Years later during his Hong Kong police training, Jonathan and his intake were taught

Cantonese, a more complicated language than Hausa. On one occasion, they were ordered to charge across the cement parade ground, guns in hand and shout 'Stop, or I'll shoot!' in Cantonese. Such are the nuances of that language that an imperceptible error in pronunciation caused them all to shout the equivalent of 'Stop, or I'll open the window!'

English and its mispronunciation led to misunderstandings in Nigeria too. In the cities, it was sometimes a good idea to leave somebody to look after your car when it was parked. With this in view, prospective car minders would hover. There was always the niggling thought at the back of your mind that not employing them might ensure that the car would be damaged. Call it a Protection Racket if you like. The car owner might say to the would-be guard 'Watch it.' The minder would often misconstrue maybe genuinely or maybe not, the request to 'Wash it.' So the owner would return to find his car not only watched but washed too and an argument would ensue about payment.

Even without any words at all there were frequent misunderstandings. In Freetown, in the days leading up to Guy Fawkes night, our bonfire in the compound grew bigger and bigger as the day approached, all of us adding to it. Unfortunately, we had not told the garden boy why we were building this huge pile. On the morning of Fifth November, when we were all out, he thought that he would tidy things up a bit and this included setting fire to the bonfire.

Aspects of the Hausa language are a delight, there being many instances of onomatopoeia. For instance, a train is a 'jirigi', a duck an 'agagwa' and a turkey a 'tolotolo.' Lacking words for modern inventions, they improvise. When planes first came to Kano they were called 'jirigin sama' i.e. trains of the sky. At a dinner party one evening, a huge dish was brought in: roasted baby pigeons, carefully arranged. They were hailed as 'dan tan tabara' i.e. son of a pigeon. My wavering appetite was swiftly doused when my neighbour remarked, 'Wacko, bats again.'

I had no particular feelings about bats when I went to Africa. I certainly had no dread. I had never seen a bat. My mother was bold with any trapped creature and could deal with mice in a matter-of-fact way. But bats became a horror to me during my time in Africa. Most nights when we were eating supper by the light of a Tilley lamp, paraffin lamp or candles, bats would swoop into the room, attracted by the light. This was my cue to run out into the garden, taking my plate of food with me. The fruit bats were so large that they were referred to as flying foxes. In one house in which we lived, the roof space was crammed with breeding bats. If we had a rare fire in the winter weeks, they would somehow wriggle through into the chimney and fall, sizzling, into the fire.

In another house, the roof occupants were amusing and not threatening. They were a family of owls, whose presence would be hidden until nightfall. After we went to bed, we could hear them above us through the flimsy ceiling board, breathing noisily.

Coming and going from the outside kitchen led to some interesting incidents. A favourite dish was groundnut soup. Made with chicken stock, it was delicious and always fairly thick. The cook would pulverise the groundnuts (otherwise known as peanuts or monkey nuts) using an empty beer bottle as a make-shift rolling pin. On wet days, the soup would often arrive at the table with indentations where huge raindrops had fallen.

One evening, when his employer was having a dinner party, a frantic cook was attempting to get all the prepared dishes taken into the house. The bachelor host had already bellowed 'Where's the b....dy gravy?' The nearest human was the night watchman into whose hands the cook thrust the gravy boat. In his army overcoat, with a large bow and a quiver of poisoned arrows slung across his back, he made a sensational entrance into the dining room.

In bush stations, there was always the hope that the company would supply a generator so that at night there would be lights. One difference from mains electricity was that it was not at all economical to keep use to a minimum. Everything worked better when the generator was run to its full capacity. Every house in the vicinity of a generator would be lit up like an ocean liner after dark. We had such a luxury for some time and the final instruction at night would be to call out of the bedroom window to the night watchman, 'Kachi moto', i.e. 'kill the engine.' All would shudder to a stop. But our whole contraption eventually shuddered to a permanent stop and was taken away to Kano for repair. It never returned. For this reason it was not possible to rely on such a fickle piece of machinery. Refrigerators ran on kerosene, paraffin. They worked on the condensation and evaporation principle. There was a metal fuel reservoir in the base. Out of this came a stout wick which was lit. The flame was sufficient to operate the cooling mechanism. The heat was carried up a tall integral chimney with an open vent at the top. The wick had to be trimmed periodically. If the length left protruding were too long, a great deal of dirty smoke would result. In a surprisingly short time, the whole house would be enveloped in a cloud of filthy vapour. So care was needed to keep the wick trim.

By day the only light in the 'kitchen' came from a slit in the mud walls which could be closed by taking away the piece of wood which propped open a wooden flap. It was difficult for the cook to see what he was doing and the heat was terrific. It was even hotter at night, with a paraffin lamp to see by. Hot from my Home Economics training, I found all of this very bizarre. The water whether from a well or a nearby river had to be boiled and filtered before it could be drunk. Water was boiled in a soot-encrusted kettle over the wood stove and then poured into a porcelain cylinder which contained two or three unglazed, porous pottery 'candles.' The water dripped through these and by means of a little tap, the boiled and filtered water could be run off into screw-topped bottles and stored in the refrigerator. Bathwater was heated in old four-gallon kerosene tins on top of the wood stove. The tins were then carried across the compound and tipped into the bath.

On my first morning in Nigeria, there was a heavy tropical downpour. The lightning danced across deep puddles. One of the less orthodox tasks of Chima, the garden boy, was to take a pot of tea across to my husband's nearby office in the mid morning. To my surprise, he appeared at the back door with the teapot wrapped in a tea towel in one hand, holding the tip of a large banana leaf in the other. The leaf acted as an umbrella. The office was an old wooden building, built on high metal stilts in order to deter the ants from eating the woodwork. Amaryllis flowers bloomed in scarlet glory between the stilts.

Ants were a pest inside the houses. Any food left about, just a few grains of sugar, or crumbs on a table, would attract swarming hordes. A deterrent was for the legs of the meatsafe and any other freestanding food cupboard to stand in little tins filled with kerosene. This worked.

It got quite cold in the winter months in the north and houses had fireplaces. There was quite a trade in women's discarded coats, which were baled and shipped from the UK. On cold mornings, workmen would wander about in women's belted Harris tweed coats with padded shoulders and nipped-in waists. Old British Army greatcoats were also popular, particularly amongst night watchmen. Most households had one of these, businesses had day watchmen too. One old retainer was completely blind but nevertheless held onto his job.

In the towns of northern Nigeria, camel trains would come in over the desert, mainly carrying salt, vital for life. Competently hobbled, the camels, their teeth usually putrid, would sit and gobble at the road sides, their bites to be avoided. Very often the camel trains would be led in by Tuaregs, a desert tribe. The tribesmen were always magnificently dressed, their robes topped by dark blue turbans. The cloth glistened as the result of being beaten, rather like polishing starched linen with a hot iron. The main trade north across the desert had been in goat skins. By the time that they reached north Africa, they became known as Moroccan leather, considered the best. The hides and skins were tanned in many towns in Nigeria, a malodorous process. Lorry loads of skins would be brought in from the bush to be bought by the various companies. Their weight was often illegally increased by the simple expedient of throwing water over the load.

I had a wonderful trousseau. There were no dry cleaners so everything had to be washable and preferably cotton. I had crisp Liberty or Horrockes frocks for the daytime and Frank Usher, Dorville and Charles Creed evening dresses. I rather cooled towards Charles Creed, though, when I heard that the spy, Mata Hari had worn a Creed suit for her execution by firing squad. My wedding dress, of cotton broderie Anglaise, converted as planned to an evening dress. I did not trust the laundering of my precious garments to anyone else so I ironed them with a charcoal iron, a strange gadget. Charcoal was packed into a large, cumbersome contraption and set alight and then whirled around and around (out-of-doors) until the embers glowed red. Although heavy to use, it was quite effective.

Life was interesting and different. During the rare dinner parties the women would withdraw to the bedroom and the men would simply make for the garden, or 'See Africa' as it was delicately put. The women would then go into the bathroom in order of their husbands' seniority.

Hazards presented themselves in different guises. I was asked to someone's house one morning, very soon after I arrived. The host had acquired a young puppy. Dogs could not at that time have an anti-rabies injection until they were six months old. The day after I had been in the house, the puppy developed alarming symptoms which suggested rabies. Diagnosis was prolonged: an animal had to die a natural death and then its brain would be sent some hundred miles south to Ibadan for dissection in the labs. As all this took some weeks, precautions could not be delayed. Immediate treatment was vital in order to avoid the deadly disease. Before this incident, I knew little about rabies, hydrophobia. It is transmitted by an infected animal's saliva entering the bloodstream of any other mammal. I had not stroked the puppy nor did I remember having had any contact with it. However, being in the same room was enough to be at risk. If the dog had, perhaps licked its own back and then brushed past my leg, saliva could have been introduced via any broken skin or insect bite.

Originally, anti-rabies injections had been in the stomach but techniques had improved by then and were given in the nether quarters. The main proviso was that no alcohol could be consumed during the two weeks' course. This did not worry me but led to some very angry reactions from the dog owner's drinking companions. But nobody refused the injections as rabies was fatal once contracted. I had a second course years later, in Freetown. Unusually, one of our dogs had a fight with an unknown dog in the bush beside our compound. She returned with a puncture wound in her neck which was surrounded by a lot of foam.

I had examined our dog to see how she had been injured. My hands were then covered with a quantity of the frothy saliva. The dog's anti-rabies injections were up to date but no risks could be taken.

Zealots played tennis and we played golf occasionally but most bush stations had no golf courses. Like many Scots, I had started to golf when I was quite young but I was never particularly interested in any sport. A few years ago I gave my bag of clubs to the window cleaner. He seemed very pleased and it was certainly a red-letter day in my life. This was why it was all the more surprising to me that I eventually took to skiing like a duck to water and hold the Guinness record as a result.

It really was necessary to have help in the house. There were no bakeries, so all bread was baked in the wood oven. There was no air conditioning and the climate was not conducive to much physical exertion. It was well known that when a wife arrived in the household, the cook and steward generally fell foul of the new mistress. After all she was in the house for most of the day, overseeing the cleaning and more than likely keeping a keen eye on the buying of food and the consumption of provisions.

A few months after my arrival in Nigeria, all servant problems were solved one sunny day when Buba Bauchi walked into our lives. The second part of a Hausa's name is that of his village or home town. Buba was short and stocky and had a jutting grey beard. We were then in our twenties and he looked quite old to us, too old for the arduous trips to the bush which my husband's job required. Buba said that he was forty-two: this was probably a guess, as there was no official registration of births or deaths. He told me subsequently that he had served drinks to the Prince of Wales (later briefly King Edward VIII) in 1929 when he was a 'small boy' (junior house servant) in Lagos. It surprised me that a young Hausaman had gone south to Lagos to work so long ago. He assured us that he was strong and up to bush travel. We took him on and he was a vital part of our lives for many years and I always held him in great affection, which was certainly not the case vis-a-vis some Europeans and their servants. He and I were both left-handed which had the bonus that sparse cooking equipment such as knives were always in a kitchen drawer with handles at the convenient side for us both.

When we came on leave to the UK, every two years or so, Buba would write to us. He could not write himself and so he employed Ali Letter Writer. Official forms were authenticated by thumb prints. This was rather a pointless precaution because it would have been difficult to verify them. When Peter Wand-Tetley was a District Officer a form was returned to him on the grounds that the miscreant's thumbprint was not clear. He said 'I'll give them a thumbprint to remember.' Removing his shoe and sock, he pushed his big toe onto the ink pad and made an impressive addition to the form.

After we finally left West Africa, our cook Buba continued to write. I would reply and send a money order, but not for more than five or ten pounds as I was never quite sure if he ever received the money. After some years, I said to my son that Buba was more than likely dead. Ali Letter Writer knew the form and could continue to milk the modest milk cow. My son said that probably Ali Letter Writer was dead too and his son was probably carrying on the correspondence.

Eventually, though, there was a long gap with no letters. Then a typewritten letter arrived from the nephew whom he had treated as a son. Buba and his wife Mairo had no children of their own. Ibrahim, who had been a childhood playmate of my son's, wrote to say that his 'beloved father' had died. He said that Buba had received all the money and he hoped that Allah would reward me in 'folds.' He enclosed a photo of himself in which he was sporting a moustache and wearing the particular headgear which denoted that he had been to Mecca.

Although it is expensive, it is the aim of every Muslim to go on pilgrimage to Mecca. Buba was rewarded by his several 'children' by their arranging not only for him to go to Mecca but for his wife to go too. This was unfortunately some time after we left Africa so we missed all the excitement. I would have loved to have known how he felt about his first journey in an aeroplane.

As well as being a Hausa, Buba was also a Fulani (rather like being British and a Scot). The main activity of Fulanis was rearing and tending their distinctive cattle. These were large white animals with humps which flopped over their necks. A frugal friend of mine cooked not only tripe from Fulani cows but also the hump, which she served up rather like tongue. Not a good idea.

The Fulanis were very decorative people who wore bright, often mirror-encrusted garments. There were fierce initiation ceremonies, rarely seen. The young adolescent boys would be harshly beaten but were not allowed to show any sign of distress or emotion. During the beating, the victim would smile at himself in a looking glass, admiring his appearance and ignoring the agony. Their appearance was often enhanced by antimony, Africa's answer to mascara. Out in bush one day in a lorry we did in fact pass a group engaged in just such an initiation ceremony.

When tending their cattle, Fulanis stand on one leg, supported by a stout stick. Their language is attractive, the main greeting being 'Jum?' (Are you well?) The answer would come 'Awali Jum.' (I'm well). Reassured that all was well, the participants would then exchange a satisfied 'Jum, jum, jum sagow.'

Before each produce-buying season, middlemen were provided with cash advances. They would then go out into the bush and buy various crops from small 'farmers.' These people would be cultivating tiny plots and eking out a living. The produce would then be transported in sacks by donkey and stored at some central point in the village. We would return a month or so later to check that the middleman had bought as he should. The result was usually satisfactory.

The distribution of cash was quite astonishing. Our normal transport was a ten-ton lorry. In the back, on the floor of the lorry, would be up to £100,000 in shillings. Coins were always used as white ants ate any paper money.

If we were setting off early in the morning, this displeased the bank manager's wife. She did not like her husband to get up early to go to the bank and issue all the money as this disturbed her rest. So the cash had to be drawn from the bank the day before travel. If we were going out to bush on a Monday, the money would have to be drawn on the Saturday. Banks and businesses were open on Saturdays in the UK as well in those days. The money would be piled in the lorry and driven around to our house.

Labourers would then carry it inside and stack it under our beds. Each calico bag contained £100 in shillings and this amount was printed on the bag. It was normal for each labourer to carry five bags on his head. Their necks strained and bulged as they carried each load into the house. I would be deputed to stay in the bedroom and to count the number of bags as they were carried in. We could not then leave the house over the weekend because of all the cash which was stashed there. This was absurd, really, as the delivery was no secret and any determined thief could have made a swift getaway.

It was not unusual for traders to owe money to the company. On one occasion my husband saw a company debtor walking along outside on the dusty road with a bag on his head clearly marked £100. This was the sum which he owed. He was on his way to the bank to pay it into his own account. My husband strolled out, greeted him and relieved him of the bag of money. The somewhat startled trader went on his way.

It was cheering, though, how honest most people were. European employees were trusted unreservedly but I remember one breach. The British bank manager of a branch in one of the towns took bribes of £60,000 from various traders to favour them before their competitors with loans with which to buy produce. He left very quickly and was said to have bought an hotel in the Channel Islands.

Before going to Nigeria my husband had been in the Bank of England. Security conscious, he decided that cash should be secure when we travelled. He had a large wooden box made. It was put in the back of the lorry and the bags of money were stored inside. He locked it with a large padlock. We then set off down a bush road, with deep corrugations in the loose laterite surface. It was a bone-shaking ride. In fact it shook more than bones on this occasion, as the box with the considerable weight of coins soon went through the wooden floor of the lorry. We limped home, where the lorry floor was repaired, the box was discarded and the money bags were distributed over the lorry floor. We set off again without further mishap.

We were always a source of great interest when we arrived in bush villages. The word would go ahead, 'cumfany, cumfany.' (Company). Groups of children would stand and gaze at us wide-eyed. Their mouths would often be wide open too, flies wandering in and out as they gazed. After only a few days in the bush, my own white limbs would look alien even to me.

Driving along any road, we would encounter troupes of monkeys. They would leap across the road ahead of us and always left a member as a look-out, crouching by the roadside until we had gone. Goats were unpredictable and would rush across in front of us, putting themselves and us in peril.

Arriving at a bush 'station' was always a relief. The day's journey would have been very hot, the road unbelievably bumpy and dusty. In the dry season we would often drive along roads which were in fact dried out river beds. When we reached our stop for the night, we would make for the 'rest house.' Out in the bush, this would consist of one large round mud hut, thatch roofed, earth floored, the 'windows', wooden or corrugated iron panels in the wall, propped open. It would be completely empty.

Alongside would be a smaller mud hut and this was the 'biyan gida' (behind the house) which stood in for a lavatory. There would be a hole in the ground. The whole thing was thatched and mysterious rustlings could be heard in the thatch, usually caused by bats.

We carried with us everything needed for about five days out 'on tour.' This consisted of canvas camp beds plus mosquito nets, a canvas bath on a wooden tripod and a canvas wash basin, similarly supported. Camp chairs and a collapsible table completed the furniture. We took bottles of water prepared for the journey, as there was not such a thing as bought bottled water. All provisions went with us. There was no means of keeping anything cool so we bought a big, wide-necked Thermos in which floated ice cubes. It did not take long for the ice to melt. This flask, amazingly, survived all our travels and was recently used to take a hot curry to the local races in the UK on a cold day.

On top of the money on the lorry floor, there would be the various bits of bush furniture and on top of this, firewood would be piled. Although there was wood galore in the bush, it was always better to start with some. There was not much room in the cab of the lorry, so Buba, our cook, bounced along uncomplainingly on the firewood in the back, clutching a live chicken.

When we reached our destination in the bush and the lorry was unloaded, the first thing that we would hear would be a half-hearted squawk as the chicken's neck was cut as was Muslim custom. Within a remarkably short time, a cloth would be on the table, the Tilley light on it hissing away and attracting many insects. The cooked chicken would appear on our plates and the evening meal would begin.

As it got darker, bats would flit by, bullfrogs would croak and the sounds of Africa, accompanied by drums, would lull us to sleep. Heat always seemed to be a great soporific. Deep sleep, though, was usually accompanied by vivid and hectic dreams so that one would wake suddenly more exhausted than on going to sleep.

I suppose all this sounds very romantic nowadays but it didn't feel romantic at the time. It left me with a great appreciation of creature comforts. One of these is the daily delivery to the house of the current newspaper. In West Africa, batches of newspapers were posted to us from the UK, initially by sea. A bundle would come every two weeks or so, depending upon the sea mail and the train north, known as The Uplimited, from Lagos. Disciplined people would read a fresh paper every day, perhaps even ironed by their 'boy' using the charcoal iron. But my impatient nature would find me scuffling through the whole lot haphazardly in order to absorb a pot-pourri of news.

Throughout all our time in West Africa, the people who worked for us in the house and garden were for the most part pleasant and unfailingly cheerful. At one time we had a West African grey parrot. It lived on the verandah in a large cage. It was able to imitate my voice and would call Audu the garden boy with great accuracy. Audu would come pounding along to answer the call from wherever he was working. Even when he saw that it was the parrot yet again, he would nevertheless double up with good natured laughter.

During the rainy season, some of our travel was done by train. The most memorable trip was soon after I arrived, when we went to Rahama by train, a station on the way to Jos. This hill station was always spoken of with great affection by Government officers who sometimes spent local leave there. But the commercial companies did not allow local leave so we never saw Jos. The journey to Rahama took place on the Bauchi Light Railway, a narrow-gauge track of two feet and six inches. The carriages were wider than the track. We had all our necessities loaded onto the train and I was dressed in some fashionable creation with a starched underslip. Despite this, I was painfully bitten by a tsetse fly, the carrier of Rhinder Pest, which afflicts cattle. On another occasion the company insurance did not cover travel in the passenger section so we sat on deck chairs in the goods van with a herd of pigs.

Part of my husband's remit was to count the stock in the various company 'canteens' and to check the account books. I would act as scribe as he counted endless bales of cloth most likely woven from Nigerian cotton.

After cotton had been bought in its rough state, it was taken to a 'ginnery' where the seeds were extracted from the cotton 'bolls.' It was then put in sacks and taken to Kano, the rail head, to wait for a train to the distant southern port. The cotton was sold to the British Cotton Growers' Association. Their stores in Zaria had an unusual nightwatchman cum burglar alarm in the form of a crowned crane bird. It would emit piercing squawks whenever anyone approached. BCGA also had a 'museum' in its UK headquarters in Manchester. It housed all the unusual things which had been found in bales of cotton. These were alleged to range from all types of clothing and belongings to human hands. Cloth was woven and printed in and around Manchester.

In northern Nigeria bags of groundnuts were stored in huge pyramids, also awaiting transport by train to the southern ports. They were famous in their day. When the Queen visited Nigeria in the Fifties, she asked if she would see the pyramids of Kano. As there was none on the Royal route, one was swiftly built. As the Queen passed it on her way to the airport we all stood and cheered as she left for the UK.

Whilst in the north, she had stayed in the residency of the governor of the north in Kaduna. The staircase had a metal bannister. The static was so fierce that someone had to stand with a hand on the rail whenever the Queen went up or down, in order to earth it. One governor had been a great trial to his staff: he rarely sat down, even on long, tedious train journeys. His staff in attendance therefore had to remain standing too. For this reason he was known as 'mai wandan kerufi' i.e. the owner of the iron trousers.

A Durbar was arranged for the Queen's visit to Kaduna, the capital of the north. My son was born there a few years later and an unusual aspect of post-natal care was that one would be woken from a deep sleep so that sleeping pills could be administered.

Health matters were uppermost for the Royal visit and all visitors to the city had to be inoculated against smallpox. Perversely, many did not require such attention as their pockmarked faces confirmed that they were immune to the disease.

Our life in bush stations was enlivened by various events. We lived next to a bachelor at one point and in the shared garden lived a large cockerel; its outstanding characteristic was that its crowing took the form of the first five notes of The Blue Danube. This was quite attractive but happened almost before dawn on most days. It lasted until one Sunday morning; the crowing began and then there was an earsplitting bang. Our neighbour had shot it from his bedroom window. So that was the end of the Classical Cock.

Highlights were when we went to the larger towns every six months or so. At the end of the produce-buying season, the small number of middlemen who had taken the money but not produced enough produce were taken to court. The nearest court was in Kaduna, which rejoiced in mains water and electricity. One bonus was that I could take the curtains and chair covers and all could be well washed. We were always short of water. It was a matter of luck whether or not a well could be sunk in the garden. Otherwise water would be carried from a nearby river. When drawing water from the river, great care had to be taken. Surface water was dangerous as it very likely contained a river fluke which causes Bilhazia, a liver disease. The water therefore had to be drawn from a deep hole, dug into the river bed. If the river was near, the water was put into cleaned four-gallon kerosene drums which were then carried yoke-like across the shoulders. If the well was some distance away, disused forty-four gallon petrol drums would be filled, brought up to the house by lorry and tipped into a tank The water would usually have dark red laterite soil in suspension. Any white garment would soon have a pink tinge.

It does not take very long for it to be brought home to anyone living in primitive conditions that there is no substitute for water. From the Wusasa River at Zaria, the lepers would dig amethysts. I took some of these back to Hatton Garden where I learnt that they were not of gem quality. But cut and polished, they still could be turned into attractive trinkets.

Recycling was a word not then heard but its practice was widespread and covered almost every item. There was no rubbish collection service and there was little need for one. Almost everything was recycled: empty tin cans were swiftly pressed into use as drinking containers. Old car or lorry tyres were cut to shape and formed sturdy 'flip flop' sandals. Empty kerosene tins were cut with tin-snips to form rudimentary stirrups with vicious spurs incorporated. Anything left would be swiftly consumed by hyenas who roamed at night. They have some of the strongest jawbones in the animal kingdom and will quickly devour any prone being.

Improvisation was ingenious. I saw a lorry out in the bush one day. A goat skin had the orifices, legs, tail and head firmly tied closed thus making a pouch which was filled with water. As the lorry rattled along, the resultant evaporation cooled the water for drinking. If a spring broke on such a vehicle, the lorry boy would leap off and cut a branch from a suitable sapling. This would be bound over the broken spring and served its purpose.

Some government officials were given their air fare but allowed to drive home across the Sahara if they wished. A friend intended to do this; he arrived at our house one afternoon having just bought a large, second hand car for the desert trip. Eager to show it to us, he put it through its paces by driving us out to his house in the bush. The electrical system failed. The car therefore had no lights so it was not possible to return home. We spent the night with him; he had a spare toothbrush. The moon was so bright that night that we could have read a book by its light.

A few days later as a peace token after our unexpected, luggageless night in the bush he left a brace of bush fowl

which he had shot. They taste like partridge. His note
read:

'The mountain sheep are sweeter,
But the valley sheep are fatter;
We therefore deemed it meeter
To carry off the latter.'

He eventually crossed the Sahara. For the desert trip
at that time, there had to be at least two cars in convoy,
each carrying four spare tyres. The authorities had to be
informed so that a light aircraft could be on hand if rescue
were needed. In a letter he told us that he had gone home
via the Hoggar route and at some point had shot duck
by moonlight. It seemed to be the same area from which
Dennis Thatcher rescued his son Mark when he went
missing during an African car rally years later.

After about seven years in the north, punctuated by spells
of leave in the UK, we heard that we were going to Lagos.
This sounded almost as gloomy as a death knell. The
south was considered wicked, dangerous and generally
inferior and decadent. Imagine my surprise when quite
the reverse was the case. There was clean, running water
which did not need to be boiled, apart from the period
when a dead man was found in the mains. There was
air conditioning in one of our bedrooms, frozen goods
were available, fresh produce was flown in daily from the
Canaries and generally there were all mod cons. The UK
papers were a mere day old.

Life was fun and we enjoyed ourselves while it lasted.
Then we heard that we would move yet again, this
time slightly further north to Ibadan. This university
town lacked the allure of the sea and creeks which we
had explored in our newly-acquired boat complete with
outboard engine.

The most unusual building in Ibadan was Bowers Tower. It stood on a hill and was reputedly built by a District Officer who had some money left from his official budget one year. The tower's main characteristic was that it had a double-sided circular staircase. On ascending, you could hear descending footsteps on the other side of the dividing partition.

Vera, my friend in Lagos, telephoned one day to ask if I would like to buy a piano. This was a pearl beyond one's wildest dreams. Someone had donated it to raise money for the Red Cross. When I said that I was willing to pay the £40 asking price, it was mine. A lorry brought it up to Ibadan. It was a battered upright with brass candleholders. Pianos were much sought-after but they fared badly in tropical climes. Their wooden cases warped in the damp heat and insects would hungrily devour the felts. An iron frame was essential.

This one had previously been in St George's Hall in Lagos. I was very puzzled as it contained quite a number of bones. But we removed these, a piano tuner came up from Lagos and it was put into working order. I learnt later that the nightwatchman at the hall had died in a ritual murder some time before and that his feet had never been found. I did not feel quite so enthusiastic about this new acquisition after that.

This was just as well as within months we heard that another move was in the offing, this time a change of territories to Sierra Leone. An Irish surgeon at the hospital bought the piano and I last saw it disappearing in an ambulance.

The saddest aspect of moving to Sierra Leone was leaving our cook Buba behind. We had a rare bond. It would have been unwise for him to leave his native land. He wrote via the letter writer, that he had been unable to eat for a week after we left. Happily, we were all reunited in Nigeria for a spell before we finally left Africa.

Just after Christmas 1965, things took a nasty turn in Nigeria. We were back in the north, in Zaria, the town where I first lived. Life was much the same as usual but things had moved on a little. Both of the bedrooms in the bungalow had air conditioning. Our son, by then nine, had already had two terms at school in Britain and had flown out for the holidays. Television was in its infancy and for his arrival I had hired a TV from the local dealer, a truly gargantuan set. The aerial had to be fixed to the roof but the correct angle to access the signal had to be found first. Garuba, the steward, went up on to the roof plus the aerial. I ran in and out of the house to tell him when the picture was getting sharper. Having achieved as near perfection as was possible, we then settled down to watch the programme. It was some time before we remembered that Garuba was still up on the roof, patiently holding the aerial. He was amazingly good tempered when he was released from what he clearly thought was yet another peculiar duty which was expected of him.

The advent of mains electricity brought some unexpected results. One householder went on tour for a fortnight. When he returned, his cook greeted him enthusiastically with the words 'The cooker never go die.' In other words, the cook had left the oven, grill and all the burners switched on for two weeks.

At the end of the Christmas holidays, early in 1966, I was not looking forward to our son's departure. The day before he was due to leave, we went into the town to stock up with anything which he could take back to school for his tuck box. Whilst in a shop, a friend came up to me and whispered: 'You won't be able to get out of Zaria. There has been a military coup. The roads are closed and the rebels are manning road blocks.' This was an unimaginable shock. We were about two hundred miles from the airport at Kano and it was difficult to get any information. We gathered that BOAC were not sending any planes to Northern Nigeria until the situation clarified. I suppose that these events could have been predicted. The prime minister at the time was a Hausa, Alhaji Tafawa Balewa, a Muslim. The Sardauna and Sultan of Sokoto were powerful figures as were many others in key posts, all Muslims.

The Christian Ibos,(Igbos) originally from the east, worked countrywide thanks to their better literacy. The Army were mainly Ibo and had clearly been bearing a festering wound of resentment against their more powerful northern neighbours. Their bitterness erupted dramatically during the Night of the Long Knives when several Ibo Army officers assassinated the Prime Minister, most of his cabinet and other northern leaders. This took place on the night of 14th January 1966 and Ramadan was fast approaching. There was no further bloodshed at that time. During the ensuing days, a curfew was imposed between late afternoon and morning.

It was never possible to telephone the UK from northern Nigeria. But, wishing to tell my parents that our son's departure had been delayed and also to allay any fears they might have had for our safety, I made an attempt to call them via the local operator. Within minutes, I was astonished to hear my father's voice. He was just as amazed to hear from me. No news of trouble in Nigeria had reached the UK at that time and my call probably raised more fears than it allayed. Two days later, with about six other families, we decided to drive to Kano with the children who were due to return to the UK.

We set off one morning in a convoy of six cars. At the first road block outside Zaria, there was a young

Nigerian lieutenant with a submachine gun. My son was tremendously excited by all of this drama and enquired in a loud voice, 'Are they the rebells [sic] Mummy?' But the rebels raised no threat and we reached Kano safely in the late afternoon. We found rooms to stay in at the Central Hotel, previously called the Rest House. It stood next to the railway station and had a small concrete dance floor. It was there, years before, that my husband had said to me: 'This must be the only place in the world where you can dance outside under the stars to the smell of trains.'

Having arrived in Kano, our next action was to try and find out what was happening. We decided to visit Police Headquarters. The guard at the end of a long drive refused to let us take our cars inside. So, a small straggly group, we walked up the long drive. One of our number said that it felt like the fall of Singapore but fortunately for us it had a happier outcome. On arrival at the police offices, we were surprised to see a European policeman whom we knew who had stayed on after Independence. He filled in such sketchy details as he knew and told us that it was hoped that BOAC would send a plane, a VC-10, for the children the next day.

After a worrying night, we drove to the airport the following morning. A friend had warned me that whilst the 'plane was on the ground armed troops would defend it from any sort of attack. She said that this action entailed soldiers lying on the tarmac with their guns trained on the plane and thus on the embarking passengers too. I was glad that she had told me. I can still see my son in his grey flannel shorts walking past the soldiers and their guns and up the steps of the plane. Having previously been dreading yet another parting from him, I can still remember the sense of immense relief when the plane took off and I could see daylight between it and the ground as he was taken safely back to the UK.

Things were then uncannily quiet for some weeks. The Hausas began to fast for the month of Ramadan. The start is signified by the sighting of the new moon. From that day, no food or drink may be taken during the hours of daylight. It is explained in the Koran that the difference between night and day is defined by the ability to distinguish a black thread from a white thread. The fasting is very debilitating. The timing varies throughout the year but it is particularly taxing if it occurs during the extremely hot, dry season. Nevertheless, the degree of self control was striking, most people carrying on with their daily work in the usual way.

By the end of Ramadan in May 1966, the Hausas realised the gravity of the terrible events which had not only robbed them of their religious leaders but had shifted the balance of power in the country. They rose up for vengeance and killed many Ibos in the north and elsewhere. Although the rioting and slaughter was not in any way directed at Europeans, if one had been in the wrong place at the wrong time things could have been very unpleasant if confronted by an African mob.

By June 1966, many thousands of Ibos had been murdered. I heard that the primitive morgue was full and bodies were piled up outside. It was a frightening time. My husband came home mid-morning one day and said that he was about to fly south to Enugu for a meeting that day and would be back some days later. I was due to go back to the UK a few weeks thence. The prospect of being left alone there in the north with a curfew and the severe disturbances alarmed me. I quickly decided that I would get on the same flight and flew down to Lagos. He went on to his meeting. After a final night with friends in Lagos, I left Africa and flew home.

We took off from Lagos at ten the next morning. I had been given some confidential papers to post to the company's head office in London when I arrived in the UK. Feeling like a spy, I slipped the envelope into my stocking top (there were no tights then). Landing at Heathrow at four in the afternoon, I stepped out into a heatwave, one of England's hottest days, hotter than it had been in Lagos. I went to the Goring Hotel and rang my parents to tell them that I was home. Just before eight o'clock that evening, I took a taxi to the theatre where I knew that Noel Coward was appearing on the London stage for the last time. There was one seat left in the stalls. Fresh from Nigeria and its lack of facilities and with a huge head of hair, I must have looked an oddity in that sleek and distinguished audience. Everywhere I looked, there was a celebrity: Malcolm Sargeant, Yehudi Menuhin, Diana Cooper, Robert Morley and many others. The show was predictably wonderful. As I fell asleep, I thought that it would be difficult to imagine a more action-packed day.

Bermuda

Chapter Four

The broad road that stretches
And the wayside fire.
Stevenson.

Who knows what trivial events store themselves away in our memories and then emerge as a spur to action. Many years after leaving Africa but before starting my own, new, writing life, I was talking to the local garage owner one day. When I mentioned that I had lived in West Africa for fifteen years, he was amazed and said: 'To look at you now, you'd never think!' This certainly made me think and shook me out of my lethargy. He had a cruel and undeserved end. Working himself up from scratch he had always dreamed of owning a Rolls Royce. Eventually he bought one. In a freak accident, the door of the car became wedged between his garage door and the building. He got out of the Rolls, hoping to remedy the situation. For some reason and in some way, the car leapt forward, running him over and killing him.

A few years on, I was in Jamaica to attend a conference with fellow magistrates from the UK. We had been invited to the island on a judicial and fact-finding goodwill trip. I went there a few days early as I wanted to write about the various tourist attractions. But I soon realised that all the obvious places had already been written about. I stayed at Medallion Hall in Kingston, so called because it was near to Government House where medals were awarded. The hotel was unusual in that it had been won in a raffle about seventy years previously. This was almost as bizarre as a man I heard about who claimed to have won his wife in a raffle. The winning of the hotel resulted in a celebrated court case. The owner who ran the raffle said that, although the lucky ticket holder had won the building, the land was not included. But a court ruled that ownership of the building deemed possession of the land.

I slept in a beautifully carved mahogany bed, very similar to the one in Noel Coward's house at Firefly. On a visit there, I met Imogen, who had been his housekeeper for nineteen years. She had greeted me: 'Hello, lady, how de day?' As we stood by the huge window in his 'Room with a View' she told me about the morning when she and her husband found their employer unconscious when they climbed in through his bathroom window. They carried him to his bed and he died soon after. His grave is in the garden near to a little tearoom which serves spicy cinnamon cakes. Imogen said: 'I'm famous.' She had met the Queen Mother, Winston Churchill and many others. But although the whole place was interesting to me, there was really nothing new there to engage readers.

I explored all the well-known tourist attractions. Climbing up Dun's River Falls was one of them. Most of my fellow climbers were from the USA. One young wife had terrible scars on her legs. She volunteered that she was one of many children from a poor peasant family in a

Eastern European country. As a toddler towards the end of WW2, she had become entangled in electric wiring which then became live. Hideously burnt, she nearly died. A relative tore up rough sheets, bound her legs and pushed her in an old pram for many miles through forbidding countryside to hospital. Against all odds, she survived.

Still hoping to find an unusual slant on Jamaica, I took a journey on a steam train up to Appletons' Plantation. There was band of strolling musicians on board who went from carriage to carriage, strumming and singing catchy calypsos. I was quite thrown by this as their leader was almost the double of Buba who had worked for us so faithfully in Nigeria. I have always been deeply affected by the thought of the plight of transported slaves. This man's presence somehow brought that dreadful history to life. Slaves took the names of their owners. In the local telephone directory, most of the names were British, many of them Scottish. My own, Grieve, was among them.

Halfway on the journey, the train stopped at Catadupa. One enterprising stall holder was Muriel. She invited travellers to select cloth and to be measured for their choice of clothing. The ordered garments would be ready to collect when the train returned in late afternoon. The little sign at her stall announced that she had made a shirt for Prince Charles on a recent trip. I couldn't resist this and a cotton dressing gown was ready for me as promised later that day. Alas, it was stolen in a robbery in South Africa. That evening I saw the green flash on the horizon as the sun set. It was dramatic, if fleeting.

Almost despairing of finding something new to write about Jamaica, it was with some relief that I read the first words of the guide book: 'Only the hardy will climb Blue Mountain Peak (7,402 ft.) for the sunrise.' I glanced around to see who these hardy might be. Without giving myself time to think, I was one of twenty two passengers in a twelve seater minibus hurtling along the road from Montego Bay to Kingston.

As the overcrowded bus whizzed along, the girl next to me rather impatiently read some steamy novel. A glimpse of her black lacy slip interested the man on her other side to the extent that she finally gave him a noisy slap across the face. The little boy on her lap did not fare much better and let out loud howls as the journey progressed.

Arriving in Kingston, I made for the rendezvous to climb Blue Mountain Peak for the sunrise next morning. At that time, the Jamaican telephone service was not very reliable so it was a minor miracle that I had been able to arrange the expedition at less than a day's notice. The previous evening I had contacted Marcia Thwaites at Pine Grove Chalets. She had promised to organise everything for me.

I sat on some steps. Egrets perched in the trees, looking like large blooms and the bats began to swoop. Eventually a car came. A long drive followed as we made our way deep into the foothills of the Blue Mountains.

A short night followed after we reached the mountain chalets. The lights of Kingston were ablaze below. A comfortable room and good food made me wish that the stay could be longer. But a very early bedtime was necessary for the 1.30 am departure. Sleep was finished around midnight when the driver decided that it was time to wash his vehicle.

Soon after, Lloyd, the experienced Jamaican guide and I set off. We were driven in a four-wheel drive, 12 gear Mercedes across the Yallahs River. The going was rough and we needed our sturdy vehicle. Through Hagley Gap we went and on to Whitfield Hall at 3,200 feet.

Even at that early hour there were travellers afoot on the paths, making their way to market. Women carried baskets laden with produce and there was a general bustle as the day roused itself. Laterite swirled about and there was a smell familiar from West Africa of dust and moist vegetation.

We finally stopped at the bottom of a clearing in the trees and bushes. It was the start of the climb. Distant lightning flashed as we got out of the van. I noticed that Lloyd carried a large knife as well as a bag of oranges. I did not know then that he also carried a walkie-talkie. This was before the days of mobile phones.

We started the climb at 2.30 am. We had six miles to go and three hours before sunrise. The first ten minutes were up such a steep and rough path that I knew that I couldn't possibly cover six miles of similar terrain. But Lloyd assured me that it was the worst part, so on we went.

Climbing in the dark was the oddest sensation: it was difficult to balance. But I soon acquired an aid in the form of a fallen branch which I used as a stick. This helped a lot. My little torch threw my distorted shadow onto the mountainside: I looked like a bow-legged dwarf, panting along. On relating the story to my son later, he said tongue in cheek: 'They must have been very impressed with all your equipment.'

A third of the way up we paused and Lloyd handed me the sweetest orange of my life. I sat down thankfully and wondered what I was doing there, in the middle of the night, climbing my first mountain ever.

There was a strange, almost nightmarish quality in plodding on, up and up in the pitch dark. I was absurdly glad of any excuse to stop and catch my breath. The sky was blazing with stars. Venus was on the distant horizon, the Plough on its back, the North Star low in the sky. As I had seen in Nigeria, the North star and the Southern cross were visible at the same time.

Eventually we were two thirds of the way up and it was time for another stop. By now I was just daring to hope that I would make it to the top and for sunrise too. We were aware that three other climbers were behind us.

It was difficult to see where we were heading. We seemed to be going around and into the mountain range. Later, on the descent in daylight, I saw that a lot of the track was better suited to mountain goats than to humans: there was a sheer drop on one side.

Finally we clambered up a little incline; we had arrived. Tensing and Hillary could not have felt more elation. Nor could they have presented a greater contrast. Lloyd wore big army boots and a Rasta beret. When packing in the UK, I had not known that I would be embarking on such an activity; I wore a Liberty hat and pink satin plimsolls.

Soon the other climbers joined us. They were three young Canadians who had found the climb just as punishing as I had. Gasping and laughing, we pooled our resources. Cough lozenges helped to swell the feast of fruit juice and chocolate. As the sun rose, it threw our shadows on to the mist in the valley behind us, with a backdrop of John Crow Mountain. It was the most astonishing sight, akin to the Brocken Spectre, seen in the Cairngorms where it has lured climbers to their deaths.

After we went down the mountain, Marcia Thwaites was waiting for us at Whitfield Hall with refreshments and congratulations. It gilded the lily of a most amazing day. Man, it was good!

Later in the day, I had a rendezvous with my UK magistrate colleagues who were arriving by air. I went to the airport to meet them. So did two Jamaican judges and various officials. I arrived at the airport first and fell in with Elva, Moses and Chrisana. They also were waiting for the London plane, meeting Auntie. When she emerged from Customs, she was wearing a large straw hat, its wide brim richly decorated with all the fruits and flowers which she must have missed whilst away in UK. A police motor cyclist sat thoughtfully picking his teeth as he waited to escort the judicial convoy. Goodness knows what my new-found friends made of it all as I finally left in a large car with a High Court judge and police outriders.

Alas, I was not as quick thinking as two of my male colleagues who swiftly ensured a pillion place on the police motor bikes. We were quite a cavalcade. Security was tight as a senior judge had been shot dead in Kingston just weeks before.

Our convoy embarked upon the most hair-raising journey. With horns blaring and headlights flashing we fairly flew along the roads into Kingston, ignoring all red lights. A sign which I had seen the previous day 'Undertakers love overtakers' sprang vividly to mind. Had another judicial procession or indeed anyone at all been coming the other way, I would not be here to tell the tale.

Intent upon retracing my WW2 journey home across the Atlantic, I returned home via Bermuda. About sixty years after my previous visit it was still the charming place which I remembered. With transport consisting mainly of boats, buses and mopeds and with a speed limit of 20 mph, life is leisurely. I was looking for a subject for an article and riding a moped, driving on the left seemed a suitable topic.

As soon as I entered the hire shop I knew that I would get hooked. First step was to select a helmet (unexpectedly big) and I casually donned it. The girl said that I would be better with the peak at the front. This corrected, I strode out to what appeared to be a powerful machine, a two stroke, two horsepower Derbi, made in Spain.

Quinton was waiting to give me the final briefing. Throttle and brake were pointed out, also wing mirrors and indicators. Before going over the top the next step was to sign insurance documents and disclaimers.

All this achieved, I then tried to heave the machine off its stand which was not as easy as it looked. 'Come on, Muscle' encouraged Quinton. With a super human effort I succeeded in bringing both fragile little spoked wheels into contact with the ground.

Into the saddle and away I went for a practice on the parking lot next to the cemetery. Everything seemed very blurred. Panic set in as I feared that I was perhaps cracking up, the final disintegration of the flesh accelerated by all the excitement.

But I realised that I was still wearing my reading glasses, needed for all the document signing. Specs removed, all was clear as I revved and wobbled away onto the parking lot.

White marble cherubs kept an eye on things. Their proximity and all the graves brought a taste of the sort of danger which lay ahead. Man's mortality, particularly mine, was close to my thoughts.

At that moment, I unexpectedly encountered Johnny Barnes, a local celebrity. He had noticed how serious and sad everyone looked as they drove to work. So when he retired, some years previously, he decided to become Bermuda's unofficial hailer. Every day, he stood on the approach roundabout to Hamilton and waved enthusiastically to every car. He was unfailingly in place from five am until 10am.

On this sunny morning, his stint over, he was strolling home. He had obviously developed nerves of steel from all those years of standing in the traffic as he hardly flinched as I rode up. We had a friendly chat and I went on my way after doing several laps of the parking lot.

By then there was no holding me. Off I sped, intent upon reaching St. David's lighthouse.

Stopping at some traffic lights presented no problem. Starting at them again was a different matter. A large sign warned not only of road works but DEEP TRENCH. This took some handling I can tell you. For a moment it seemed that I would miss the surrounding road and plough along down in the trench, only the crash helmet visible and my neck below, match stick like. But they don't call me Schumacher for nothing. The skill gained over the years on the roads of many wild countries – Nigeria, Scotland – came to my aid. I cracked this problem and went on my way.

The road across the island is called the Khyber Pass. My mind clicked into dramatic mode. This was just as well as rounding a steep bend, I met a large horse and its rider straddling the highway. Quite a moment. The rider was not helmeted and was also on his maiden ride. In fact, between the three of us, only the horse knew the ropes. He turned his head and clopped away through a conveniently open gate. I don't know what happened to the rider after that but I do know that this steeled me for any eventuality. Talk about white knuckle riding.

I took the road for St.David's and stopped some miles on at an attractive craft shop. On saying that it seemed a bit isolated, the owner looked at me in some surprise and said that many customers walked there from the Southampton Princess Hotel. It was my turn to look startled. As far as I knew, the hotel stood at the other end of the island. The owner was too tactful to say that I had foolishly taken the wrong road and kindly suggested that someone had turned the signpost around. Retracing my steps, I went on and was by this time hungry and very thirsty. The temptation to down a couple of cans of Bermuda's national drink Dark 'n' Stormy (black rum and ginger beer, delicious) was almost too much for me. But the thought of the headline: 'British magistrate on Bermudan criminal charge' made my choice more moderate. They still have the death penalty in Bermuda and that makes you think, doesn't it?

So I pulled up at Bailey's Food D'Lites and ordered a sandwich. A sign suggested that I 'Spend a day in Bailey's Bay.' But I had wider horizons in my sights.

At last I whizzed up to the lighthouse. It was closed. This was just as well as, on dismounting, I found that my shaky legs barely held me.

Next destination was St.George's. Past Lovers Lane I sped, basking in the scent of oleanders, the sea a wonderful blue. Lovers scattered in all directions as I rode by. No, I made that bit up: they had already headed for the bushes. I treated myself to a little tour of the town, down Shinbone Alley, past Ye Olde Towne Deli and along One Gun Alley.

The monthly event of Beating the Retreat was about to begin. I just had the time and energy to climb up the steps to the verandah of the pub in the square. Dignitaries were still arriving as darkness fell: a vicar in Bermuda shorts, the Mayor next to a brigadier.

The 'Bonnets of Bonnie Dundee' rang out in the starlit night, as did 'I Could Have Danced all Night' which was how I was feeling by then. When it was all over, the flag lowered and the Last Post blown, all that was left was the exhilarating moonlit ride back to base. Paul Revere had nothing on me. Singing at the top of my voice, I sped past startled bystanders.

Quinton tactfully expressed no surprise as the bike and I returned unscathed. Laughing in the moonlight, I gave him a brief resume of my ride. He grinned hugely. I did too.

Montserrat

Chapter Five

For there are good things yet to do
And fine things to be seen
Before I go to Tokyo
By way of Aberdeen.

'What size feet do you have?' asked kindly Mr. Kabori from the Japanese National Tourist Office. When I divulged the information, I could almost hear him reel at the enormity at the other end of the telephone line. I could not help thinking of Fats Waller's 'Your feets too big.' Mr. Kabori gave a deep sigh and said 'It is not possible.' This was the culmination of months of planning. The Daily Telegraph had accepted my idea of an article on skiing in Japan. All plans had been made and I was due to leave in three days' time. I could see the whole venture slipping through my fingers because of this unforeseen problem. Mr. Kabori merely wished to ensure that everything would be waiting for me when I reached the ski resort. Some quick thinking saved the day. I said 'But I could wear men's boots.' I could hear a politely stifled scoffing chuckle at the suggestion. With no idea at all of Japanese ski boot sizes, I had clutched at this last straw and he was eventually persuaded that this was in fact a feasible solution.

First there was a ski press trip to Aviemore and I planned to go to Tokyo directly after that. Unusually, there was heavy snow when I left by train and it was touch and go whether I would be able to get north at all. The day had a poor start as the car park where I had hoped to leave my car was for season ticket holders only. The British Rail man then went on to tell me that the train that I wanted to catch had been cancelled. When one did come along, I would have to change twice before getting even as far as the main line station. He finished by saying to me with some satisfaction: 'It's not your day, Miss.'

The snow was banked high at the sides of the track and by the time that we reached the next stop the station lamps were wearing huge snow helmets at rakish angles. I decided at that point that it is certainly not better to travel hopefully, it is much better to arrive.

Once in Aviemore, there was a short meeting for all the journalists on the trip. It was interesting to hear about setting up the infrastructure for a ski resort: you buy a ski lift off the shelf. Getting it delivered, by helicopter and installed is quite a different matter. I am always surprised to see that the supporting pylons are not perpendicular but look as though they have been hauled earthwards with a huge tug.

The Aviemore pioneers were a determined lot. Continental resorts have far more snow and its arrival is reliable too. Scots had to be very single-minded if anything was to come of their dream. Aberdeen ski club was closely involved. This was during the time the James Bond film 'On Her Majesty's Secret Service' was being made. One winter, the club members were staying in Murren, where the film was being shot. Sleeping in a sort of dormitory, they were roughly woken one morning after a night on the tiles. A scout from the film company was looking for skiing extras and had heard that these young blades were in town. But the young blades were hung over and very sleepy and nobody took much notice. But a few minutes after the scout left, they came to their senses. Somebody said that he thought that he had heard that they would be paid X pounds and that a helicopter would be involved. Everyone then suddenly woke up, dressed hastily, pulled on their 'tackety' boots and ran down the village street after the film man.

They were engaged as skiing extras, goodies and baddies. Unrecognisable in all their ski gear plus hats and masks, they nevertheless watch the film whenever it is shown, nowadays with grandchildren on their laps.

Next day, when we met to tour Aviemore's slopes, there was plenty of snow. But the wind was whistling down from the Arctic in seventy-nine mile an hour gusts. It was necessary to point parallel skis straight into the wind on the Poma lift to avoid being blown off the track. Going up was very uncomfortable with icy pellets pitting our faces. Breasting the ridge at the top of one drag, my companion and I were suddenly blown backwards into a heap. One journalist displayed the most admirable tenacity. I met her as we skiied along and I thought that she had had a nose bleed, her face looked like a lurid red type of primitive face painting. I admired her for carrying on skiing in spite of it all. That evening, she confided that she had not had a nose bleed but, in the rough conditions, had jabbed her ski pole up a nostril. This made her perseverance even more laudable.

Before ski lifts were installed at Aviemore and the Lecht, when there was a brisk wind some enterprising enthusiasts used parachutes to get themselves blown up to the top of the mountain. Bought from surplus kit shops they were designed to carry equipment weighing about a hundred pounds. With one of these strapped to your back and with the wind in the right direction, you were soon transported up the hill. The parachute would then be gathered up quickly and the air knocked out. One skier was bowling up a hill in this way when he passed a man who was walking. Before either of them realised what was happening, the surprised man was enveloped by the silk folds and had to be extricated.

Travelling to the mountains is much improved now. In the past, the road into Braemar would be closed by snow from December until May. Gangs of forty or fifty men had to hack out huge blocks of snow in order to open the road which had to be accessible by the first of June when the fishing and shooting parties arrived.

It can still be an inhospitable area. On the hill paths you can quickly and easily get disorientated. The Grey Man of Cairngorm is still imagined eerily on Ben Mc Dhui. At nearly three thousand feet, walkers on misty days encounter the phenomenon. You imagine that you hear footsteps behind you. When you stop, they stop.

Walkers have been lost by being deluded by this, moving forward confidently, assuming they are on firm ground and then plunging down an abyss to their deaths.

One of the routes up Glenshee and around the Devil's Elbow was notoriously difficult and hazardous in the early days of motoring, even on fine summer days. This is Britain's highest road with a gradient of one in five. As a small child in the early thirties, I remember going around the Devil's Elbow in the dicky (called a rumble seat in USA) of my grandfather's car. With my brother and cousins, I sat in the hinged seat outside the back of the car, far from an adult's reach. I cannot imagine why we did not all fall out, jousting about as children do. But the dicky was quite deep. We never had a mishap and fared better than another brother and sister. As their mother's Fiat rounded a particularly sharp bend, there was a juddering jolt. The dicky snapped shut, trapping the tiny occupants inside. It was some time before the distracted adults realised what had happened.

My father spoke of journeys around the Elbow between the wars on motor cycle trials. Later on, he drove an oil-cooled Belsize Bradshaw car. It had twin cylinders. When the oil heated it carbonised and caused great problems with burnt out valves. The next car which he drove on that route was a Hampton which 'went like the wind' at forty miles an hour on the flat.

The first buses to drive around the Elbow were open topped charabancs. The passengers had to get out and walk on the steep gradients. Reverse gear was lower than first so the buses would back up the road. As they were long, it would take two swings at the bend in order to get around. Other drivers, sitting on the dyke waiting for their own cars to cool down, would form an audience.

Driving was on rough surfaces, radiators boiled, gaskets blew and clutches slipped. Often, brakes and hand brakes would not hold and a cautious driver wedged a brick under the rear wheel when stopped. Parking could be at an angle against a wall and this too prevented the car from slipping backwards if the brakes failed. Radiators had to be topped up halfway around the Elbow so the prudent carried a can of water.

There is a sad little marker at the roadside just south of the Devil's Elbow. In the nineteenth century, a gypsy girl ran out and was run over by a carriage. Even today, there are usually bluebells and heather at the spot.

Between the wars, near to the Elbow, a Miss Greta Gordon walked to meet a friend halfway between their two houses. Caught in a blizzard, her frozen body was found days later. Recently, when an old sheiling caught fire, it took three hours for the fire engine to battle through. By the time that they arrived the building was just a shell.

After WW2, cyclists travelling from Perth to Braemar found the route extremely taxing. They would have been making for Youth Hostels and their 'push' bikes may have been Triumphs, Humbers and Raleighs. Even in the eighties, the route down looked a whole lot more tempting than the route up.

The road was straightened out when the Braemar to Blairgowrie route was improved. Now drivers cruise along hardly noticing a rise until they get to the 2,199 feet Cairnwell pass.

In the early days of motoring, a warning of trouble ahead could be given by an AA patrol man in khaki jacket and breeches. Riding a motor bike with side car, he would not give his usual salute. The AA member then knew that there was a hazard ahead, perhaps a police speed trap.

The press trip over, it was time to take the sleeper south from Aviemore to Euston. There was no dining car on the sleeper and I told the sleeper attendant that I was very thirsty. He said ' You'll get a cuppie the night, lass.' In Scotland a cuppie refers to tea. A woman is affectionately called a lass for all of her life. When he brought the cuppie to my compartment, knowing that I had been skiing, he asked if I was using some linament. This was not the case and did not say much for the perfume which I had been wearing at the farewell dinner an hour or so before. It was the attendant's final run before retirement after twenty-two years. He had always worked on sleepers, saying: ' I'm an owl.' Indeed he looked very like an owl with protruding wings of hair, a missing top front tooth and descending canines. A friend had given me a sleeping pill which I lost so I spent the rest of the night looking for it, exploring all the intricacies of the bunk straps and a bit of dust too.

A bus from Euston took me to Heathrow and I was all ready for Japan. Mr. Kabori had abandoned his desk in Piccadilly to bring my tickets to the airport. He had already sent an itinerary to me, written in English. I was going to spend a day or two in Tokyo where an English speaking guide would show me the sights. I would then make for the slopes on my own. On this final meeting, I fortunately asked Mr. Kabori to add Japanese characters next to the English instructions. I would have been sunk without this. Few people in Japan spoke English at that time, but I was able to point to the Japanese characters on the itinerary and taxi drivers knew where I wanted to go.

The huge white leather seat on the plane ensured a comfortable journey. In the next seat was an aloof Japanese businessman who was visited frequently by a subservient employee, eagerly hoping that all was well. I woke in the night to strange sounds. The mogul was clipping his fingernails, fragments flying in all directions. I think that he was probably not impressed by having to sit next to a Western woman. He chose to ignore me.

I was going from east to west on both the outward and return journeys which would take me right around the world. As we flew over the north pole, bound for refuelling in Alaska, we were told where our silver aluminium survival suits were stored in preparation for any emergency landing at or near the North Pole. I was entranced by Alaska after my first glimpse of it from the air.

Landing at Narita, Tokyo, exposed the first cultural difference. A planned rendezvous on the 'first floor' turned out to be at ground level. Although this term also applies in the USA it was new to me at the time. Using a handkerchief is frowned upon in Japan and instead sniffing is acceptable. I was told that a lot of water is wasted in Tokyo by the modesty of the women. When they go into a public loo, they always first flush it with water so that the sound of the refilling cistern will cover their own activities. This has resulted in twice as much water being used than is necessary. The solution has been to install tapes of recorded running water in each cubicle. The occupant presses a button and modesty is preserved.

My hotel room was on the seventeenth floor. The window would not open and I felt claustrophobic. A rechargeable torch was fixed to the door jamb. An accompanying notice said that, in the event of fire or earthquake, a wet towel should be put over the head and then one should crawl to the nearest exit or stairway, staying at floor level in order to be lower than the smoke. I checked where the fire exit was.

Everything needed for the night was provided, including a kimono and cloth slippers. There was a little heater for making green tea. The weight of the water in the pot activated the electric ring on which it stood. The bathroom was a capsule, standing in the main room. Tooth brush and toothpaste were provided.

During dinner in the hotel that evening, I seemed to be swaying about and put that down to tiredness. But I subsequently realised that Tokyo is prone to frequent earth tremors and I was experiencing one.

In the coffee shop the next morning I was confronted with teeny little chairs and tables. It was like being back in kindergarten, my first 'Dame' school with Miss Robertson and Miss Reid. There was a relief map of the world on the wall, Japan in the centre. I looked up to the top left corner, where I expected to see the British Isles but there was a blank space.

I had time for a brief visit to a court. There were no juries. The retiring room of the High Court judges overlooked the grounds of the Royal palace.

The only oriental judicial system that I had heard any thing about previously was when my son was in the Hong

Kong police. An intriguing story did the rounds. A man, charged with some misdemeanour, appeared in court. He alleged that he had been mistreated by the police. When the judge asked what form the ill treatment took, the man replied that he had been held upside down by his ankles out of the window of the multi- storeyed police station. The judge found this difficult to believe. The defendant said that he could prove that he was speaking the truth. Whilst he was being dangled outside the window, he had written his name on the wall. With that, the judge, advocates and the defendant all went off to the police station. Sure enough, on the wall, upside down, was the hapless man's signature. I wondered what sort of pen he had used. Most varieties would not write at such an extreme angle.

Next morning it was time to take a taxi to Tokyo's railway station. Not only can taxi drivers open the passenger doors by means of a lever but they can close them too. Lace antimacassars adorn the seat backs. The price is clearly displayed on a meter; there is no tipping anywhere so the journey was simple. I waited for the Shinkansen (The Bullet Train) at the appointed place and the carriage with my pre-booked seat in it drew up at that exact spot.

It took a long time to pass through Tokyo's suburbs, so long that it seemed unlikely that we would reach the station for the ski resort at the advertised time. But soon we emerged from a tunnel and there was a concerted gasp as snow-topped mountains came into view. A transfer bus took me to the hotel.

I was surprised to learn that there are over six hundred ski resorts in Japan, ranging from the Japanese Alps on the main island of Honshu to those on Hokkaido. The latter, known for its fine powdery snow, has been the site of Winter Olympics. I was heading for Naeba, just two hours' journey from Tokyo.

The resort was dominated by a 3,500 bed hotel. The summit of 5814 feet is swiftly reached and there are several log cabin style restaurants. This purpose-built resort is truly a triumph of concrete art. The slopes bear a substantial spider's web of lifts and related machinery. The plentiful snow was barely visible through all the metal.

Little English was spoken but the receptionist understood my simple needs. So I was kitted out, wearing men's bright red boots. Women's boots were white. Not only was I considerably taller than most people on the slopes, I stood out dramatically in the large, almost luminous boots. Strangely, there seemed to be no beginners, everyone skiing along quite expertly.

The restaurant at the summit had cosy log fires. Choosing lunch posed problems as none of the food looked at all familiar; the menus on the wall were in Japanese. I ordered some soup-like liquid being enjoyed by a man nearby, followed by what looked like ice cream but turned out not to be as no dairy food is eaten in Japan.

The slopes were very crowded during the day. High speed four-seater lifts moved two thousand people an hour to the top. The single-seater ski lifts were an eye opener. Not only was there no safety bar but there were no sides or backs either. It was like sitting on a little tin tray. How children were persuaded not to hurl themselves off I did not discover.

Skiing was down only one face of the mountain. I skied cautiously as I did not fancy a seventeen hour flight home with a limb in plaster.

Then it was back to the hotel for dinner. This consisted of Clam Chowder and Cuban lobster au gratin with noodles. The first course reminded me of Rupert Brooke's verse

'If you were like clam chowder
And I were like the spoon
And the band were playing louder
And a little more in tune,
I'd stir you till I spilled you
Or kiss you till I killed you,
If you were like clam chowder
And I were like the spoon.'

After dinner I experienced floodlit night-time skiing for the first time. It was invigorating in the crisp night air. Trendy young bloods from Tokyo take the Shinkansen to the nearer resorts straight from work. They then ski at night and take the train back to the city, some skiing for most of the night and returning in time for work the following morning. In the hotel, there was no sign of any apres ski clothes. Everyone seemed to wear their designer ski wear throughout the day and evening; there was much strolling to and fro to display the clothes. Some devotees of the sport wandered about the hotel with their up-to-the-minute skis slung over their shoulders for all to admire. The swimming pool was popular although there was a sign which banned diving and tattoos, the latter favoured by many Triad members.

The next morning I watched an aerobics class on the bedroom TV. I joined in for a bit but went back to bed after a while, worn out with all the activity.

Crossing the vast plains of Russia during the flight home the next day, there was a straight line below us for most of that stretch of the journey. I foolishly did not ask what it was. I thought at the time that it might be the tracks of the trans-Siberian Railway but it has also been suggested that it might have been the route of the Tract.

Soon, another of my suggestions for an article in the Daily Telegraph took me to Canada to cover the Calgary Stampede Rodeo, established in 1923. An annual event, it originated from cattle being rounded up for sale in the city. As with previous trips, the authorities thought that they would make the best of a British journalist's visit. Despite my protestations that I could not use the material, a trip to the Montreal Jazz festival was included in my itinerary. Before going, I went to London to get some suitable clothes. I made for the city's largest store. Liftmen were still employed at that time. The Sales were on and the store was very busy. An empty lift arrived, the doors opened and I got in. To my surprise the doors closed immediately, ignoring all the other waiting customers. We were off. Having previously been jostled in an overloaded lift despite the warning notice on its wall, I said to the liftman that it was a luxury to be in such an empty lift. He replied: 'I haven't got time for that lot to make up their minds where they want to go.' I said that in that case he must go up and down empty for most of the time. He said 'I do, mostly.'

On the bus from Montreal airport, I chatted to a fellow passenger, a well dressed young man, as I did to others on the bus. I checked in and made for my room on the ground floor. As I was about to put the key in the lock, I looked around and saw that the young man was beside me. I asked what he was doing. He replied 'Madam, we are companions.' I said that we certainly were not and he went away. When I got into the room, I rang the reception to tell them what had happened. After that I was escorted to my room each night. Even so, every time that I went into the bathroom after that I would yank the shower curtains open, expecting to find a band of beknifed brigands in there.

The jazz festival was predictably fun. Montreal surprised me, though, as so many of its inhabitants apparently spoke only French. The Cathedral guide, for example, didn't speak English. It didn't exactly encourage tourism. As I had not been back to Canada since I left in 1943, I went to Toronto. There I met Betty with whom I had shared a desk at school all those years ago. She had been married and had two children and owned a flower shop in Chicago. About twenty-five years before she had gone to the island of Montserrat on holiday. She fell in love with the place and bought a house there. That was the end of the flower shop and that phase of her life. When I met her, she had been living happily in Montserrat for a long time; her daughter was married with a son there and they ran a successful real estate business. She urged me to go and visit her and this I promised to do.

But in the meantime I continued my journey to Calgary. The whole city was en fete. The main activities, apart from those in the ring, seemed to be eating breakfasts, all of which were free. The largest recently hosted thirty-five thousand people. But first of all one had to don the obligatory white Stetson and acquire a swagger and a slightly bow legged stance to indicate years in the saddle. The Stampede kicks off with a two hour street parade including marching bands, gigantic floats, pipers, a twenty-seater bike, Mounties, clowns cart-wheeling along and all the fun of the fair. This is all followed by two weeks of 'the greatest outdoor show on earth.'

In days gone by, after the annual cattle round up, the last man back to town bought the drinks, hence the accompanying races watched by thousands in the arena. There was daring bare-back riding, great feats in the saddle, calf roping, bull riding where the rider is fortunate to finish with just a black eye, steer wrestling and chuck wagon racing. The race starts with four wagons per heat, each drawn by eight horses racing around the outside track accompanied by four outriders. Hooves and dust fly as the crowd roars its encouragement.

After all the day's excitement, the local joints are truly jumping, beer is swilled from the bottle, everyone dips into big plates of nachos and sour cream and dozens of hot air balloons take off all over the city whilst the earthbound enjoy energetic line dancing and the two step. As they say, you go in as a stranger and end up with a ranchful of friends.

Back home again, it was time to try and arrange a trip to Montserrat. By then the first catastrophic eruption of the volcano there had taken place.

Antigua was my jumping-off point. I was in one of the many smart resort hotels around the island. Not only did I have a little private beach but also a sea grape tree. The fruit was new to me and delicious. All the fruit was wonderful; for the first time I tasted a truly ripe pineapple, a tiny, very sweet variety. Conk (the local name for conch) was on the menu. The mollusc lives in the pink, curvy shell which sounds like the sea when you hold it to your ear. There were bright blooms everywhere. A mongoose scuttled by one day; he and his mates had disposed of any snakes long ago. It was sheer luxury to dip into the balmy sea and then to stroll along the beaches. This was a refreshing change from Mexico. I had recently been to Acapulco and discovered that the beach there is strewn with shards of broken glass, a legacy of all the beach parties.

Bound for Montserrat on the Antilles Express, we sped past the hotel where I had stayed and the waiters and waitresses stood on the terrace and waved white tablecloths. Maybe they thought that I would never return. The girl next to me on the boat wore a canary yellow peaked cap and matching T-shirt. She looked like the Caribbean song 'Yellow bird.' But the jaunty resemblance ended when she turned to me and said despairingly: 'Gone, my house has all gone.' Her first return to the island a week before had confirmed the wildest rumours and her worst fears.

Betty met me at the new jetty at St. John's, on the north of the island. Whether it will in time welcome cruise ships there as Plymouth had in happier times, remains to be seen. Before the Soufriere volcano erupted, Montserrat was dubbed the Emerald Isle. It had abundant fresh water and was the source of most of the produce for the surrounding islands. We did not see any evidence of the eruption on the drive to Betty's house. The villain of the piece, 2,000 feet high Castle Peak, had not even been the highest point of the Soufriere Hills. They had been a tourist attraction before the tragic events, their fumaroles venting puffs of foul smelling smoke. The Soufriere range extends around several islands. I saw similar fumaroles on a subsequent visit to Guadaloupe.

A dinner table set for eighteen stretched the length of Betty's verandah. Everyone at the party remembered the chronology of the volcano's activity. Nobody forgets the night that changed their lives forever. The combined noises of the Amazon, Mississippi and the Nile could not match the volcano's violent roar. Copious debris was thrown out every second, rising to twenty thousand feet and then falling back to earth. Dust masks were not introduced at first because the dust was not deemed to be dangerous. Opinion soon changed. This was not before householders in undamaged properties woke daily to find at least two feet of ash on their verandas which they shovelled off.

One of the guests told me that he had taken six months off work in order to dig the foundations for his large family house. By the time that I met him, the house was completely buried, all its contents lost. 'We had nowhere to take anything.' It is difficult to grasp what it must have been like. Everyone was in the same position. It was not possible to whistle up a removal van. Many inhabitants left the island but a substantial number of stalwarts remained.

Next day, the deputy Police Commissioner took Betty and me down to Plymouth. We were lucky; any heavy overnight rain would have filled the deep gullies and washed away hopes of any vehicle getting there. A scene of unimaginable devastation greeted us. We were walking on a crust of compacted lava dust which was at least fifteen feet deep. Most two storeyed buildings were buried to roof level. Rivulets of water were hot. Boulders the size of cars were strewn about; a two hundred gallon petrol tank lay crushed on its side like a discarded Coke can. The prison was a twisted wreck, the prisoners all rescued.

In 1902, after Mt. Pelée erupted on nearby Martinique, the only survivor was a convict, incarcerated deep in a dungeon. Who says that crime does not pay? After the Montserrat eruption, thieves, knowing that a great deal of money was still in a bank vault, tunnelled through the wall of an adjoining building. They escaped with the money but one of them left his jacket behind, with his wallet in the pocket. When they were captured, the problem was where to keep them securely. The governor of a nearby British territory did not want any more villains than he already had and the problem was still unresolved when I left.

There were incongruities in the ruined Plymouth. Every structure was wrecked, sturdy iron girders twisted like spaghetti. And yet, in a little yard, the top of a metal clothes pole protruded, the washing line and two wooden clothes pegs still intact. A piece of ornamental wooden 'gingerbread' carving hung from the eaves of a house.

There was not a blade of grass, a bird, a cat or any living creature. As in 'Burial of Sir John Moore at Corunna':

> *'Not a drum was heard,*
> *Not a funeral note.'*

The only living being on the island which could predict the volcano's activity was Betty's dog. I placed a short account of his activities in the Daily Telegraph. Trembling with apprehension, the dog had spent the previous Christmas Day cowering in the bath. On Boxing Day, the volcanic dome collapsed, sending twenty five million cubic metres of built-up magna crashing down in fifteen seconds, rolling over already evacuated areas including five villages. It continued for a mile out to sea. There were no lives lost on that occasion but nineteen people had already died. They had ignored warnings and had returned to their properties maybe to feed or rescue livestock.

A further twist to the island's misfortune was that since Hurricane Hugo in 1989, nobody had been able to get insurance. Everything was uninsurable and uninsured.

The return journey on the Antilles Express was wild. It was not until we had powered back to Antigua that the enormity of what had happened hit me. Antigua's brightly painted houses, vivid flowers, market stalls and streets crowded with tourists must be as Montserrat's had been prior to the eruptions. The ruins which I had seen that morning were all that remained of Plymouth, previously Montserrat's bustling capital.

It was shortly after my trip to Montserrat that I was asked to give talks, with slides, on cruise ships. On one trip we headed for Corunna, one of the home ports of the Spanish Armada. Remnants of the invaders escaped the English fleet near the Firth of Forth and fled on north. Most of the ships were wrecked, one still lying at the bottom of the sea near Tobermory. But several came to grief on the north east coast of Scotland and there were survivors. My mother's family were reputed to be among them and her maiden name, Torrie, has a Spanish ring. My interest was rekindled some time ago when watching a 'Travels with my Camera' programme on TV. The story featured Cadiz, also a home port of the Armada vessels. In the course of the documentary, cameras went into a house and interviewed a number of women. I was dumbfounded as they were doubles of my mother and her sisters, with high cheek bones and dark hair. Modern DNA testing could confirm the link.

After that, the voyage became quite dramatic as we crossed the Bay of Biscay. A technical problem brought the ship to a halt. It was in the middle of the cabaret, the soprano singing some impassioned song. There was sudden silence. One passenger said 'You'd think they would have let her finish her song!'

Initially not alarmed, I went to bed. Hours passed. There were few announcements and no ventilation or lighting. It became uncomfortably hot. I began to think that perhaps we might in the end have to leave the ship. I decided which possessions it would be vital to take with me. Foremost were the hundreds of irreplaceable colour slides needed for my talks. Next came the keys to my car, parked at Southampton. After many hours we were on our way again and all was trouble free from then on.

On the mantlepiece in my bedroom as a child there was a photograph of my father standing in the garden of Reid's Palace Hotel, Madeira. He had often talked about his time on the island but the rest of us of his family did not feature in his reminiscences. Shortly before he died, I asked him about it all. He started 'Well, lass,' and went on to explain. We were living in Lisbon in the early thirties.

He was with I.C.I., had a watching brief on the company's agent in Madeira and sailed there periodically. Having completed his morning's work with the agent, he then stayed at Reids for thirteen and a half days until the ship returned. I remembered this when we sailed into the harbour at Madeira. Armed with the photograph I made for Reid's. I found the spot in the garden where the picture had been taken decades before. Only when I reached the place did I realise that my father took the picture himself. There was a wall of appropriate height where the camera would have stood. He always had the latest gadgets and I realised that he would have used a camera with a delayed shutter. My father knew George Bernard Shaw and had had tea at his house at Ayot St. Lawrence. I never asked how they had met. But there is a photograph of G.B.S. at Reid's, dancing the Tango. Presumably, that is where my father met him. A mystery was solved.

Moscow, unfinished

Chapter Six

'Like Webster's English dictionary, I'm Morocco bound.'
Bing Crosby

Having seen Russia from a great height on my way home from Japan, I was soon on my way there. Erna Low, pioneer of ski packages, was invited to Moscow by Valentina Tereshkova, the first woman in space, who had started a scheme whereby British tourists would stay with Russian families. Their payment in sterling would be invaluable to their hosts. In return, the British would be looked after by a family who would show them many things of interest that might not otherwise be possible. Erna was interested in promoting this form of tourism and she asked Eithne Power, a prolific journalist, and me to go with her. I collected our visas from the Russian Embassy in London, walking along the little road beside Kensington Palace in the spring sunshine.

A few days later, we headed for Moscow on an Aeroflot plane which had been bought from Danair. The passengers were a mix of nationalities: Indians, a tall bright-eyed Magyar in a turban and also Phil Ryan of 'The Animals' who soon produced his guitar and sang to Erna. He and the group were going to take part in an open air charity concert in Red Square which was shown live by satellite across Europe and along the West coast of America.

On arrival we three were taken to the Hall of Deputies and lengthy formalities were waived. Soon we headed off in a large car to Valentina's dacha in the country just outside Moscow. We passed bendy buses, towering apartment blocks, women in headscarves, fishermen by the rivers under large shade-giving umbrellas. Ornately carved wooden houses lined parts of the route; there were factories and avenues of birch trees. About fifteen miles from the airport, we reached the dacha in cool beech woods in the Barvikha region. The property was enclosed by a high, green painted metal fence. Two Alsatians roamed at night amidst the roses, lilac and peonies. The only remaining contents of the forbidding-looking but now disused guardhouse were two squashed Pilsner cans and a dismantled radiator. It was peaceful and quiet, only the rustle of the trees and birdsong to be heard. In this privileged area, the Brechnev family were close neighbours.

The dacha belied its humble name. The substantial mansion had been built by a former Mongolian ambassador whose wife was Russian. The exterior had an Oriental flavour, the interior was luxurious and comfortable to the extent of having a sauna and a sumptuous room in which to relax afterwards. Vases of lilies-of-the-valley scented the rooms. Wherever we went in private places, there was exquisitely fine and beautifully decorated china.

We were looked after by ample and affable Luba who had been a ballerina. Her husband Valentin looked as though he had stepped straight out of 'Uncle Vanya.' We were given blackcurrant tea and little alphabet biscuits. Most dogs which we met had English names and Jimmy, their poodle, was no exception.

We had already met Valentina Tereshkova in London when the trip was being planned. She told me that, prior to her journey into space, she was forbidden to tell even her mother that she had been chosen. On the day of the flight when neighbours heard the broadcast news, they flocked to her mother's house. Mrs. Tereshkova insisted that there was some mistake as her daughter had told her that she was spending time at the local parachuting club. Eventually she was convinced that it was indeed her daughter hurtling around overhead. Valentina said that it was tremendously exciting, Earth so beautiful from afar. She persuaded the authorities to allow her to stay in space for an extra day. I asked if she had managed to sleep. She said that there was so much to do during the day that she slept well.

On our first day in Moscow, we were taken out to Star City, the space headquarters. Luba blew kisses to us as we left. There was a traffic jam on the way with much overheating of car engines, a black poodle panting frantically out of the window of the car next to us. Our driver was so enraged by it all that he shouted at a nearby pedestrian. The pedestrian in turn was so annoyed that he picked up a loose stone to hurl at the driver.But by then we were moving.

At Star City we met Aleksey Leanov, the first man to walk in space. He took us into a replica of a space craft and explained its workings. There were no beds, just a little curtained-off alcove, where he stood and closed his eyes. With weightlessness, there is no need to lie down to sleep.

Lunch was in the cafe at Friendship House. A 'babouska' wearing a headscarf was clearing the tables. She soon came and gave us glasses of mineral water and bright green cordial. Afterwards we walked through an underpass where artists displayed their paintings and florists sold bunches of gladioli. The eternal flame burned near the wall of the Kremlin; there were formal beds of tulips; white and dark lilacs were everywhere. A bride and groom with their attendants came swinging along, all beautifully and stylishly dressed. This was in contrast to the austere goods in the shops.

Outside Lenin's tomb, all was hushed, only the quiet footfall of the soldier guarding the building was to be heard. It was shut. In the wall behind were the ashes of heroes including Gagarin, the first man in space. I thought of newsreels of the past which had shown the might of the Russian military machine when tanks annually rumbled through Red Square on 1st May. There was a limpid blue sky and the swallows swooped. I sat on a curb near to the tomb and started to do a quick line and wash sketch of nearby St Basil's Cathedral. But the sentry moved me on. The scarlet sun had dipped behind the buildings, its last rays reaching the fantastic domes. I wrote in my notebook: 'For pure romance, it must be Moscow in May.' But then I was told that, so determined was Ivan the Terrible that the cathedral should never be copied or bettered, that he arranged for the architects responsible for its construction to be blinded.

Dinner that evening was in a restaurant in a leafy square with black painted railings and impressive statues. Our host and his son were millionaires from Turkmenistan. On the green baize tablecloth were cut glass dishes with mounds of glossy caviar, jellied sturgeon, hors d'oeuvres and meats with pickles. Afterwards we ate cherry ice cream. We drank to 'Success' with copious glasses of vodka and champagne.

Then it was time for us to board the sleeper to St. Petersburg. As elsewhere in the country, the railway station was an architectural gem. The immaculate night train matched the station. There was a wide corridor and varnished dark wood. We were seen off by Vladimir, one of the first observers appointed by the United Nations. He had spent his boyhood in Siberia where his military father was stationed. Eithne's and my compartment had two beds and there were mirrors, hangers and net holders for our various possessions. We had been warned to look after our purses and bags. A fellow passenger, an American girl who had been working in Moscow for four years, was jostled by a gypsy woman whom we had noticed earlier and who stole her wallet.

A few minutes after seeing us off, Vladimir came back. Although we knew that it was necessary to lock our compartment from the inside, we did not realise that it would still have been possible for thieves to open the door. They would rob and even murder the occupants. Vladimir showed us a little bolt at the top of the door which can be secured from the inside.

This reminded me of an experience of friends. They met in India and were married in Calcutta Cathedral. Travelling on the night train up to the hill station of Darjeeling for their honeymoon, they were unable to book a double compartment. The bride booked a 'Ladies' only' compartment. The bridegroom had to share with a wealthy Indian who was travelling with a large dowry of jewels and money for his daughter. At the first stop, our friend changed compartments and joined his bride. All went well until the train arrived in Darjeeling when it was discovered that the wealthy Indian had been murdered and all the valuables had gone. Not surprisingly, the finger of suspicion pointed at the bridegroom. He was taken off for questioning after a 'Kukri' was found in his luggage. Eventually he was absolved. Thieves had evidently known about the wealthy passenger and had climbed along the roof of the train and into the compartment. Had my friend not already left, his new bride might have become a widow before the honeymoon even started.

Our Russian train of twenty carriages slowly started to move. We stood at the wide open door space, a big gap between the platform and the train. There was a creak as we slid out of the station into the moonlight.

Russian music woke us as we sped past flat, green fields. We reached St. Petersburg with no murders or mishaps. Beatrix was our guide, gentle and chic with delicate bones. She was an architect and had designed buildings in Siberia, Volgograd, Leningrad, and Omsk. Her mother was Georgian and her father a Romanov. Beatrix said that they were both much stronger than she as they were well fed as children. She was from Azbaba, intriguingly twinned with Albuquerque in New Mexico.

The Hermitage lived up to its reputation, containing even surgical tools used by Peter the Great, who fancied himself as a surgeon. His patients may not have been volunteers, though. His dental forceps sent a shudder down our spines. He also designed ships and drew the original plans for St. Petersburg, which is built on forty-two islands and has three hundred and sixty bridges. The railings on the bridges are of many different designs, intricate and lovely.

There were dramatic paintings in the Museum of Russian Art. A vast work, showing naked children being forced into the Coliseum by Roman soldiers, their frantic parents clutching fruitlessly to save them, lions slavering in the background, was one of the most chilling which I have ever seen.

St. Nicolas' Cathedral, with its five gold domes and low-ceilinged, candelit interior had a wonderful atmosphere. Climbing the two hundred and forty steps up the outside of the dome of St. Isaac's gave a great panorama. Waiting to fly back to Moscow, we were apprehensive when we heard that an Aeorflot plane on an internal flight had crashed. Always optimistic, Eithne commented 'Perhaps it's just a scrape.'

Searching always for somewhere different to write about, I heard that there is skiing in the High Atlas Mountains, Morocco. Again, the Daily Telegraph said that they would take a piece from me. Again, all doors opened.

As I set off on the trip, nobody knew that it was my sixtieth birthday. But no sooner had we taken off when the Captain said over the Tannoy: 'Will Mr. Norman Rowlerson please make himself known to the crew.' This was odd, surely I did not have a masculine namesake? By the time that a second announcement was made the stewardess had arrived with her trolley. Showing her my passport, I asked if perhaps I was Mr. Norman Rowlerson? Indeed I was. As I was a guest of the charter airline, she asked what would I like to drink. It was only ten in the morning but I thought that I should celebrate my birthday. I asked for a small bottle of bubbly. I do not normally drink much alcohol. It went straight to my head. I spent the rest of the flight lisping tipsily to the man next to me that I was going to Morocco to ski. He looked surprised.

On touchdown there was quite a scrum to enter the airport buildings. As soon as we got inside I heard the announcement: 'Will Mr. Norman Rowlerson please make himself known to the airport staff.' Still feeling a bit light-headed, I reeled up to a uniformed figure and said who I was. He sprang to life. To my embarrassment I was ushered straight through all immigration and customs, past the crowds of waiting people. A long limousine then whisked me off to an hotel. I was asked to leave my passport at reception.

Having had a short nap and regained my faculties, I dressed and went down for dinner. I ate alone (when I recounted all this afterwards to my mother, she said, in a reprovingly Scottish tone: 'I should think so too.') I had finished eating and was just leaving the dining room when all the lights went out.

It was my first time back in Africa since I left Nigeria. In the darkness, I said to myself that things really had not changed much at all. But at that moment the kitchen door swung open and out stepped the chef in his tall hat, bearing a cake groaning with lighted candles. He made for my table. I was astonished. What great PR – my birthday had been picked up from my passport at reception. Most of the other diners were French, I knew nobody and I could cheerfully have dropped through a hole in the floor. I think that there was some clapping, maybe even an attempt at singing. I was urged to my feet to cut the cake and it was distributed to the other tables.

Next day it was time to make for the snows. The first ski school in the country was founded by a Frenchman in 1932. We were heading for Oukaimeden which at over ten thousand feet had some worthwhile runs. Nearby Mount Toubkal is Morocco's highest peak but its terrain makes skiing impossible. Abdul the driver arrived to collect me and we set off at a hair-raising rate. There was quite a lot of traffic on the road, ranging from lurching lorries to daintily stepping donkeys. He was a disconcerting driver as he turned to look me full in the eye when speaking to me. Wishing to impress me with his diligence, he announced that he was very experienced, a real workaholic who drove for twenty-five hours each day. I reflected that mercifully he was a Muslim and therefore presumably sober.

There are several ski areas in the Middle and High Atlas and there can be snow from December until May. The High Atlas rise near Agadir on the coast and extend northwards for over four hundred miles on their way north east near to Taroudant. They pass the strange phenomenon of climbing goats. When vegetation is scarce, the goats, nimbly climb even thorn trees to eat the sparse foliage.

The drive from Marrakesh to Oukaimeden was to take about an hour and a half but the driver was clearly out to break all records. Starting on the plain the road started to wind up towards the mountains which were soon in sight.

I suggested a stop for coffee at the French owned Ourika Hotel. I hoped that perhaps this would break the driver's hell for leather approach to the journey. The view was lovely, the sweet scent of mimosa hinting that Spring was not too far away. The pit stop in fact fuelled the driver up for even more daring driving. We hurtled along beside churning rivers filled with snow melt from the mountains.

Little Berber villages clung to the slopes, everybody brightly dressed and muffled up. Soon there was snow, children pulling each other along on home-made sledges. Eventually there was a toll barrier across the road. We were there.

Whether we would ever get back to Marrakesh in one piece was far from my mind as I staggered out of the car and went off to investigate what ski equipment could be hired. The quality was poor. There was a small selection of very old skis. As far as I could see, they had been neither sharpened nor waxed for a long time. They had probably served a full life in some European resort before they were sold second hand to Morocco.

There were no other skiers about. The first haul up the mountain was by a Poma drag lift, one of four. It was manned by Berbers in khaki Balaclava helmets, an incongruous sight. With no grooming of the pistes, the snow lay in great lumps. At the top of the first slope it was almost impossible to move along at all. The only chair lift, very old and made of painted metal was nearer to the summit. Only one face of the mountain was suitable for skiing. The highest run was called The Combe of the Dead. The runs were steep, rocky and narrow. Mount Toubkal seemed just a hand's reach away.

As I went up the second stage of lifts, there was a group of Berbers, smoking nonchalantly and waiting with the Blood Wagon. In the event of any accident or injury, I am not too sure what would have happened after that. I was by then very conscious, as I had been elsewhere, that I did not want to return to UK with a broken limb, in plaster. Some years later I broke a leg in Austria. All that I had imagined about having a leg in plaster was correct. For at least six weeks, you cannot drive or get into a bath and it is a thoroughly inconvenient business.

Reaching base again, I made for the Ju-Ju bar which produced a tasty omelette. Flushed with success I was more relaxed on the journey back to Marrakesh. Abdul and I parted on friendly terms.

That evening, a danceur de plateau appeared. I had no idea what to expect and saw the most amazing act. The dancer, in Muslim dress with a small cotton skull cap, balanced a round brass tray on his head. On the tray was a metal teapot, glasses, cups and lighted candles, all unattached. He then began his act and was like a Whirling Dervish. None of his gyrations dislodged any of the objects. On and on he went, more and more daring, lying down and then standing up, turning, twisting and dancing in time to the music. Quite astounding.

Engine hut, Chacaltaya, Bolivia

Chapter Seven

'....walked the ancient ruins of the Andes'
Peter Sarstedt

I did not exactly walk the ancient ruins of the Andes. But when I suggested to the Daily Telegraph that I could ski the Andes at a great height, they liked the idea. So off I went to Bolivia. There are some mighty mountains in those parts, huge Andean crags. Because of the proximity of the Equator there is no snow under 1600 feet. My goal in South America was multi-peaked Chacaltaya in the Cordillera Real in Bolivia. Towering to 18,850 feet, it provides the world's highest skiing.

Bolivia is not a destination for flying into one day, making for the hire shop, clapping on boots and skis and heading for the slopes. At those lofty altitudes, acclimatisation is an important factor. Timing, too, is all. The Club Andino, established over fifty years ago, runs the 'lift' which at that time operated only on Saturdays and Sundays. I allowed a few days to get used to the altitude and to do some undemanding sightseeing before attempting any more strenuous acitivity.

I was high enough already without going near any mountains. At 12,000 feet above sea level, La Paz (Peace) the country's largest city, lies in a deep bowl almost two miles across. The airport, up on the Alto Plano, is 15,000 feet high. A doctor friend, used to high places, suggested that I took the drug Diamox. When I went to my G.P. and told him that I was going to ski at nearly 19,000 feet, he said 'You're mad!' When I asked why, he said that I might die. As I was unconcerned about this he gave me the prescription.

Advice on acclimatisation came from another doctor who had practised in La Paz for some years. She said 'Do nothing for the first twenty-four hours.' I thought that I knew what that meant until she added: 'Don't even unpack.' This really made me sit up and think. It was good advice, though. Some travellers require an oxygen boost as soon as the plane doors open. When I landed, the man next to me was gasping for breath by the time that we reached Customs. As he was young and healthy looking, I wondered if this was maybe a ruse to draw attention from some doubtful import. Women who have borne children, no matter how long ago, acclimatise best. Their bodies have at one time supplied an extra one with oxygen and apparently remember the knack. Certainly this worked for me.

Arriving at the Hotel Gloria late on a Tuesday afternoon gave a few days to draw breath, literally. Feeling a bit apprehensive, I went to ground in my room with a large bottle of mineral water and a fat paperback. Tea, consisting of a teabag dangling in a cup of tepid milk, was brought to the room. My main concession to non-exertion was to use the hotel lift. Periodically, lightning flashed over the rim of the city but, disconcertingly, no thunder could be heard.

By the time that the day arrived for the pilgrimage to the mountain, I had learnt a lot about Bolivia. This is the land of unexpected superlatives, with Titicaca the world's highest navigable freshwater lake, the airport the highest on the highest plateau. The Incas were the first to produce silver. On the ancient terraces around Titicaca over a hundred varieties of potato were cultivated. In 1931, the lake was stocked with salmon trout from Canada; there are Rainbow trout farms, kingfish and catfish. When Jacques Cousteau dived there he discovered the world's largest frogs. Whether this pleased his French gastronomic taste is not recorded.

Deciding to have a look at Lake Titicaca, I took a bus to the little port of Huatajata. Sitting on the bank was a Bolivian woman wearing layers of petticoats and a bowler hat, tipped at an angle. She was spinning alpaca wool by the same primitive method used by our cook's wife in Nigeria. All that is needed is something like a child's spinning top and plenty of patience. The fibre is teased and wound onto the revolving spindle. Vicuna are the smallest of the llama family, their wool and that of alpacas being much in demand. The larger llama has evolved as a pack animal. They all eventually join the food chain.

An old hydrofoil took seventeen passengers along the lake, forty five percent of which lies within Bolivia. Being very deep, it never freezes. It can however get very rough. But it was calm on this day. I was glad of that because I had heard an alarming rumour that, if someone falls into the water, it is traditional to leave them to drown as a sacrifice to the local goddess.

Our guide, Jesus, assured us that all would be well. I had decided, rather reluctantly, not to go to Puno, Peru, at the far end of the lake. There had been a few unpleasant incidents there and I did not want any delay to prevent my producing a good piece for the newspaper. So the rest of the travellers waved brightly as they continued on their way having dropped me off at Copacabana. Rio's famous beach takes its name from that remote spot.

I was free to wander the streets of the small town before the return trip in the evening on the hydrofoil. Always fascinated by cemeteries, I headed for one on the hillside. Marigolds grew in abundance on the grave of Josephine Espinosa. I gathered some seeds. Taking them back to the UK quite legally, I scattered them around my seaside garden in the north of Scotland. They bloom more profusely every year. They are a reminder of an inscription on a gravestone in Glen Esk, Angus, which reads:

'The grave, great teacher, to one level brings
Heroes and beggars, galley slaves and kings.'

The church in the town is dedicated to the Virgin of Copacabana. It is said to be the only church of Moorish design in South America, all the others being Baroque. In the early seventeenth century, Philip the Second of Spain sent an Augustinian priest to build the church on the site of an Inca temple. The altar is elaborately decorated with fine Bolivian silver and seventeen carat gold. Intriguingly, the altar has a reversible Madonna: the figure can be turned around so that it faces into a little chapel behind the main church.

There is an annual gruelling pilgrimage on a nearby steep hill, the Calgary of Copacabana. Zealots climb barefoot and more often than not they crawl. The entrance to the cave, their goal, is so narrow that if you are too large to enter, you are damned. So you have the choice of going on a diet or facing eternal damnation.

After lunch at the hotel, I could probably have entered the cave with no trouble.

I had been shown with a flourish to a table with an off-white cloth. The first course was of various raw delicacies. I chose the soup of coarsely chopped vegetables, which was hot and tasty with rice in it. Then there were three little crispy trout fillets served with semi-cold potatoes.

The sweet was an unwashed orange cut into quarters. I topped it all off with a bottle of mineral water.

The street market was a colourful riot of many strange things. Amongst them were llama foetuses which are buried in the foundations of any new house. The whole thing reminded me of Noel Coward's song:

'Yams and clams and human hands
And vintage coconut wine,
The taste of which is frightful
But the after effects divine.'

The women are prolific knitters and use very fine circular needles. Their bowler hats are made from blocked felt toques, imported from Italy. I bought one.

I felt a little vulnerable being at such high altitudes and a long way from home. Nobody knew where I was staying. So, for the first time ever, I decided that it might be a wise precaution to sign the book at the British Embassy. When I got there the First Secretary said that he was about to make his weekly visit to the infamous San Pedro jail. It was well known that anything could be found there, guns and drugs being no exception. He asked if I would like to go with him. When he said that no British citizens were being held there but that he was going to see an Australian, for some extraordinary reason I said that I would not go. It is one of my few regrets. Perhaps I did not want to appear voyeuristic.

The next thing that he said was that H.E. would like to meet me. We had a pleasant talk and the Ambassador asked me to the World Cup football match which was being held in La Paz the following evening.

We arranged a rendezvous. The opposing team from Uruguay had arrived just the night before. As the highest point in their country is no more than 600 feet they were at a serious disadvantage. The stadium was packed to capacity with a crowd of 50,000. The grass on the pitch was littered with pieces of paper which must have made it rather slippery. The referee was Venezuelan. Never at any time was there any sense of fair play. The Uruguayan team were pelted with missiles as they ran on to the pitch. There was continuous clapping and shouting. Everyone there seemed to have a whistle and these they blew almost as often as they breathed.

I was glad that the stadium was made of sturdy concrete. Maybe this would ensure that it did not collapse with the weight of the crowd or catch fire from the many fireworks being set off. Toffee apple vendors and popcorn sellers walked between the rows carrying buckets of ice crammed with cans of Coke and orange juice.

VIVA MI PATRIA UNA GRAN NACION was picked out at the side of the pitch in Bolivia's national colours of red, orange and green. I wrote in my notebook: 'The Uruguay goalie looks just like Dave, our milkman.' This did not do him much good as he was pelted with oranges when he stopped a goal.

Antonio Portugal of Club Andino had previously told me that the lungs of the locals are a third larger than those of other nations, achieved after years of living at altitude. The Bolivian team certainly gave their opponents a run for their money. A supine figure was carried off. The referee took no notice. Like Lazarus, the victim rose bravely from the stretcher. The girl next to me leapt to her feet and shouted instructions on play.

Many devotees had radios clapped to their ears. Uruguay's goalie got a massive boo as he deflected the ball from the goal mouth. Then the Bolivian goalie developed a terrible limp, rolling on the ground in exaggerated agony. He crawled onto a convenient stretcher. He was a hero the next moment as he got up and kicked the ball bravely, to tremendous applause. The crowd went wild. Someone fired a starting pistol. An orange hit me on the back of the head. Bolivia scored two goals and the crowd erupted. Then Uruguay scored: this was greeted with silence. Bolivia missed another – the crowd was dismayed. There were more casualties. Someone in the front clapped unsportingly as a Uruguayan fell to the ground.

Whistles blowing, the noise increased all the time. 'Our Man' nearly got to his feet twice, using binoculars to see an expected goal. As the end neared, the great roaring increased and to it was added the explosion of truly deafening rockets.

When the match was over and the defeated visitors were booed off, there followed a Mexican Wave. I had always wanted to be involved in this so I stood up at the appropriate moment. It was a relief to be driven away with H.E. in his car and off for dinner.

My companion told me that alcohol brings unpleasant side effects at high altitude. He had drunk only about six glasses of wine in his first month there. Also, as high altitude is inclined to distort one's values, it is easy to become detached from the seriousness of danger.

The drive next day to Chacaltaya from La Paz took about two hours. Soon we had driven up to 15,000 feet on the Altiplano. This is a desolate region, with dusty donkeys wandering about and a ragged dog still wearing a carnival collar from the previous week's fiesta reminding onlookers that every dog has his day. Geese waddled in and out of the mud buildings.

Suddenly in the distance there was a great snowy mountain range, the peaks pink-tipped in the sunshine. Snow had fallen on the tufty grass and we were on laterite. The road was built about twenty years ago to give access to a government meteorological station.

I was driven and guided by Bernado Guarachi, Bolivia's leading climber and a crack skier. A wiry Tensing-like figure, he stopped our vehicle halfway and produced a flask of warm Mate de Coca. This is an infusion of leaves of the same family as cocaine. Considered a specific for altitude sickness it tasted like a mixture of lawn clippings and blood.

It was on one of the many hair-raising bends that we encountered an accident. A bus, also bound for the skiing, was lying on its side but nobody was hurt or even surprised by the mishap. We rescued a bowler-hatted cook. Transferring unconcernedly to our truck she sat stoically clutching a striped bundle which contained the provisions for lunch, her skirts fanned out around her. The remaining passengers stayed to heave and push the ancient bus and eventually joined us.

Our sturdy vehicle saved us from overturning. All the same, we slithered on the precipitous bends, where the loose laterite was topped with ice. That was the last hurdle on the road to the ski Mecca.

We parked, or perched, on a little plateau next to the ski day-lodge. Lake Titicaca glinted in the far distance. A tourist was wandering about with an oxygen cylinder strapped to his back.

The peak is egg-shaped and skiing is possible down just one area, measuring less than a kilometer. The primitive lift was installed over forty years ago by Club Andino. The engine hut balances on rocks halfway up the side of the slope. From it runs a steel hawser which drops to the base of the run, then over a pulley to the summit and then back to the hut. This loop is driven by an old Ford V8 engine. A T-bar is provided for each skier to carry. This consists of a piece of wood about nine inches long. To the centre of this is tied a six feet length of rope with a hook at the end. The idea is to wind the rope around the waist, securing it by twisting around the wood. The hook is then attached to the moving hawser. Hooking themselves onto the hawser, skiers are winched to the top. I watched as students from all over the world tried, fell and tried again. They would get up and start the wearisome business over and over. Even fastening the six clips of the boots had left me feeling breathless and headachy.

As in Morocco the snow was heavy and lay in wet chunks. There was no piste as such and no grooming equipment. Progress down the slope was consequently slow. I was not alone in stopping every three or four turns to take gasps of air. The Bolivians scored with their larger lung capacity.

Stopping at the winch and turning with ski tips pointing up was quite an effort. But the prospect of overshooting and having to climb up the slope concentrated the mind wonderfully. When my turn came the engine broke down briefly. Maybe they stopped it deliberately for me. Willing hands helped to hook me up, the engine started again and away I went. I could feel the wood slewing round and the rope eventually came loose from my waist. I managed to hang on to the greasy wire. Reaching the summit, I was relieved to hurl myself onto the soft snow and a photo was taken of this doubtful triumph.

After the skiing there was great camaraderie around the wood fire. There was also a large selection of steaming socks. One footsore backpacker was glad to be given mine to wear for the rest of his trek.

The rescued cook produced piping hot soup. Zealots were there from all over the world. A keen Finn had arrived via Moscow, Shannon, Newfoundland and Cuba. Even my route had been via Miami, Panama and Santa Cruz. There were young bloods from Australia, Austria, Denmark and many other countries. Flushed with success we all exchanged addresses and became friends for life.

Soon it was time to go back to Africa. Still searching for unusual places to ski, I had heard that the Drakensberg Mountains in South Africa were a likely spot. Receiving an enthusiastic response from the newspaper yet again, a trip was swiftly arranged. As on other occasions, the local tourist office lost no time in arranging an extensive trip, most of which bore no relation to skiing at all. Before long, the itinerary arrived. Not only did it take in skiing, it included ballooning at dawn over a game park after a night in the lodge there, sailing in Durban harbour and also some gliding.

From the plane in the early morning, Africa presented an ochre landscape with hills, good wide roads and homesteads. The temperature was just 30F. A stuffed zebra gave me a startled glance at the entrance to Arrivals. The day warmed up a bit during the drive from Jan Smuts Airport. The atmosphere in Johannesburg was rather tense and it was not recommended to stray far from the hotel.

I did not stray, but was ready early on the first morning, to be driven out to the game lodge by the balloonist and his wife. At that time, there were only fourteen registered balloonists in South Africa. The first two hundred miles from Johannesburg heading north west were on a good road. We soon passed attractive houses of Cape/Dutch design with weaver bird nests hanging from the trees, acacia thorns and poplars.

The game reserve covered twenty thousand acres. The lodge was attractive with log fires, animal skins on the floors and a grand piano. There were bunches of freesias on little inlaid tables. The roofs were thatched and the walls whitewashed.

We heard that recently, at another game lodge, a woman had rung reception to say that there was a large lizard in her room and would someone please come and help. She appealed to them three times but the manager was in no hurry because he thought that it was probably just a little gecko. When they finally investigated, however, the diminutive woman was pinned into a corner by a giant iguana.

Dinner that evening included eland stew which I suppose is akin to venison. Outside was a floodlit watering hole where the animals came to drink at dawn and at dusk. We sat in a semicircle under the blazing stars. Five a.m. saw everyone dressed and breakfasted when the pilot appeared and said that it was too windy for a safe take-off He added that there are old pilots and bold pilots but no old bold ones. We drove instead in an open truck and saw game: a lion with two cubs and a lolloping giraffe complete with its young. At large in the reserve were oryx, buffalo, impala, gemsbok, sable and hyenas. On the lake were thousands of flamingoes, strutting along on their fragile pink legs. The outing ended with a braai, a barbecue breakfast.

Next day I was collected by the couple who were to take me gliding. Passing Soweto on our way out of town again, all seemed calm and peaceful despite the recent disturbances. We crossed the Vaal River, the border of the Transvaal and the Orange Free State.

The pilot had been gliding for thirty-eight years. He first flew solo at Grangemouth aged sixteen and went on to be a National Gliding coach in UK. So I was in good hands.

In order that everything could be handled by just two people, he and his gliding partner, also a pilot, had made a portable winch which they could tow to mountains and deserts, on safaris anywhere. With a cable, the glider could be winched up to fifteen hundred feet in forty seconds. A Slingsby T 21B, the glider was made of spruce and Irish linen, designed in 1942 and modified in 1946. The cockpit was open, the pilot and passenger sitting side by side. We strapped ourselves in with sturdy seatbelts, a bit like prize fighters' belts. I usually write notes but on that occasion a small tape recorder was more practical.

We were pulled up quite fast by the winch and there was a sickening lurch as the line was unhitched from the glider and the tow fell away with its own parachute.

Our climbing angle was forty to forty five degrees and we were rising fast. It seemed very high to me but the pilot said that we would go higher and try to find some thermals. No flight goes higher than five thousand feet. It was all quite alarming. The pilot explained that one must always be alert to all that is happening around you, looking for helpful signs such as flags blowing, birds, sparrows feeding on small insects, cloud, smoke and bits of paper.

We were drifting at thirty six miles an hour, dropping six feet a second. Then he tilted the glider over and explained that it is just like riding a bike, you just tilt with it. I had never been so frightened in my life. He assured me that we could not blow upside down as we were like a pendulum and would always move back to a stable position. At six hundred feet above the ground we were buffeting. I remembered the film about breaking the sound barrier when the doomed pilot said 'I'm buffeting, buffeting.' Having gone higher and not found any thermals, we landed. I was much relieved until the pilot said: 'We'll go up again and see if we can find any.' Frightened as I was, it seemed churlish to refuse. So up we went again, this time no less terrifying than the last. Thankfully, we never found any thermals.

Next day when transcribing from the recorder into my notebook, I heard my voice, high pitched with fear, say:

'I'm a bit frightened.'

Pilot: 'That's OK, you can hang on to me.'

Later, Pilot: 'We'll just go a bit higher and get some thermals.'

Me: 'This is quite high enough for me.'

'There's the winch down there,' (says the pilot, brightly).

Me: 'I can't look down.'

Pilot: 'Do you suffer from vertigo? Vertigo people are usually OK.'

Self: 'I don't suffer from anything.' Then, hopefully but not sounding very confident: 'I'll get used to it soon...' I never did.

The next leg of the trip was a scheduled flight across to Durban in order to go to a sailing school. This was just as superfluous to my article as the gliding but you have to enter into the spirit of the thing. The sea was incredibly rough, our frail little sailing boat the only one out in Durban harbour. The vessel was a Bermudan rig. Thirty-four feet long, she was built in Capetown and launched three years previously. A normal voyage might last about twenty one days, the trip from Durban to Mauritius taking eighteen. I remembered the chauvinistic phrase that nevertheless always made me smile: 'In Mauritius, fish are ten a penny and women are ten a fish.'

I was thankful that our marathon was just for the day. We were told that air always flows in an anti-clockwise direction in the southern hemisphere. I wondered about this. I had always heard that water flows down a plug hole in a different direction in northern and southern hemispheres. Living once in a house which straddled the hemispheres, a friend said that he had never been able to prove this.

In Durban, the prevailing wind is south west. I was clad in foul weather gear. This was enough to start the stomach churning before even stepping aboard. We were told that this was a proper ocean-going yacht, not like some caravan where you might sit down cosily for a cup of tea. In oilskins from head to drenched toe, I was hitched to the boat by way of a clip in case I got swept overboard. Again, it was frightening, much more so than the many small fishing boats I have been in off the north east coast of Scotland. Those, however, have nothing as effete as a sail. This boat had a nineteen horse power engine but it was for emergencies only.

As soon as we set sail, I realised why the young man from the tourist office, my guide, magnanimously decided to forgo such a wonderful experience. On these press trips, one is always driven around and generally looked after by someone from the local tourist board. I had an amusing time once in New England. I was staying in Stowe, Vermont. Having skied locally on the first day, next morning I was collected and driven to Killington, to ski there. Next day the ski resort of Sugar Bush sent another young man to drive me there for more skiing. On each occasion we passed an old-fashioned country store, complete with pot-bellied stove, hot coffee and lots of goodies. At my suggestion, we went in there each morning for a coffee. Each time I was with a different companion. In the end, the golden oldie behind the till said: 'Where are you getting all of these young men? I'm gonna follow along behind of you.'

However, there we were in Durban, in weather so wild that we were tilted right over on our side at times and I was able to look down straight into the bottom of the ocean, expecting to join Davy Jones in his locker at any moment. In better conditions, we could have hoped to catch barracuda, tuna, salmon, crayfish and many other varieties of seafood. Overhead there would have been petrels, cormorants, the great winged albatross and others. But no birds flew on that day.

I spent the night at a beachside hotel before heading north the following morning for Pietermaritzburg and another game lodge. The sun rising out of the Indian Ocean woke me abruptly. The boats had already been out to inspect and empty the shark nets which were stretched along the coast in order to ensure safe bathing. The Australians were the first to install shark nets, protecting Sydney Harbour from 1932 onwards. Durban followed in 1952, the nets standing in forty feet of water. In 1964, the Natal Safety Bathers' Association was formed. The nets there are mainly made of a flat polyethylene braid and twine. They called the knot used a half English, which will not slip. I have noted that the same knot is used worldwide from the north east of Scotland to Hong Kong and Jamaica. It seems a bit like the invention of the wheel: did the knot evolve in each local place or did early sailors spread the skill?

Before leaving Durban, I left my unlocked case in the locked bedroom as I went quickly downstairs in order to settle up a few extras on the bill. Returning, there seemed to be a lot of activity in the corridor outside my room. Prominent was a large canvas container in which the used sheets were stacked. I thought nothing of all of this. In fact most of my clothes had been stolen and apparently were in the container too.

On that day's drive there were signposts to Rourke's Drift, Ladysmith and Mafeking. I have an old recording of my father describing how the news of the Relief of Mafeking reached Montrose. As a small boy he was in church one morning with his father. Before the service began, the beadle walked solemnly up the aisle and handed a note to the minister who then announced to the congregation: 'Ladies and gentlemen, by the grace of God, Mafeking has been relieved. God save the Queen.' There was no service after that and my father ran happily out of church.

We visited botanical gardens; at Kingsmead Cricket Club was the statue of Dick King who rode non-stop the five hundred miles from Durban to Grahamstown for reinforcements in the Anglo Boer wars.

Then it was on to Pietersmaritzburg, rightly proud of its City Hall which is the largest red brick building in the southern hemisphere. Pantiles for the roof were baked on the spot. Jacarandas and bauhinia bloomed in profusion. St George's Church is still remembered as the spot where the Empress Princess Eugenie came to take her son's body home. There was time to visit and sit in on a case in the Regional Court. A woman was sitting knitting, her companions on either side helping with the tangled wool. The defendant, her son, elected to remain silent. He had allegedly stolen a pick-up truck at penknife point. The owner had suffered an open wound in his cheek that required stitches. The defendant was sentenced to three and a half years' imprisonment: he had previous convictions involving weapons. He expressed no surprise. His mother went on knitting. I have noticed that, at the time of conviction or sentence, or both, it becomes clear whether the accused has been justly treated or not. An innocent person would surely shout out or make some protest at being wrongly convicted and mercifully this seldom happens.

Nearby, the weeping Cross is another landmark, made with wood from Dellville. So many South African soldiers were killed there that for seventy two years, the cross is said to have 'wept' every year in July. The bar at Nottingham Road was frequented by troops of the Forty-fifth regiment of Sherwood Foresters during the Bush Wars of 1874. From there we could see that there was snow on the Drakensberg Range of mountains. A huge, jutting, impressive, basalt range, they are thus named as their jagged shapes look like rows of dragons' teeth and also because the fossilised remains of a three-toed dinosaur were found there. Spanning three of the four provinces of the republic, they form a stunning barrier between Lesotho and the North Eastern Cape. On we went to Umtanga through fields of sugar cane.

At Karkloof, one of the great successes has been to save the white rhino from extinction. I nearly reached extinction there myself. The guide had already driven me very close to a couple of rhino, grazing contentedly but keeping mean little eyes on us and our open vehicle. We kept inching alarmingly closer and closer. Eventually we backed away and I felt mightily relieved. Next, at the guide's suggestion, I went with him on foot across some scrub. There was a dense patch of bushes and undergrowth nearby. He suddenly seemed to change his mind about the manoeuvre and suggested that we head back to the vehicle. When we were safely inside he apologised profusely, he had not realised that there were buffalo in the bushes and we had been in some considerable danger.

My guide seemed to have had some extraordinary experiences. He once was escorting a party of six Austrian tourists who were very formal with each other, Herr This and Frau That. They were very correctly dressed in lederhosen, felt hats complete with feathers, with walking sticks and cameras. When they arrived, they were emphatic that they did not want to be taken to see any elephants as they had been charged by an elephant on their previous safari, ten years before. They got into the open truck and started off. The first animal which came along was a huge elephant which stampeded past. The guide looked around and there was not a tourist in sight, they were all under the seats.

The week progressed without further incident. No other elephants appeared. The tourists were still very formal with each other. On the last day they asked if perhaps they could find an elephant after all so that they could take some photographs as they had certainly not taken any during their previous encounters. It was decided that it would be best to get out of the vehicle and walk to where it was known that they could observe an elephant in its usual haunt. Unbeknownst to the guide, another party of tourists in another vehicle at the other side of the valley were doing the same thing. It is clear that the elephant got wind of the first party. It took fright and plunged into the bush and then charged along in the direction of the Austrians. In the lead, the guide raised his elephant rifle. Unfortunately he tripped on a root and fell on his back on the path. The roaring elephant charged past. When the guide scrambled to his feet, there was again not a tourist in sight. They were all up in the trees, hats, cameras and sticks all scattered. Aged between sixty and seventy and not particularly fit or agile, they had all nevertheless hurled themselves up the trees. One of the women was twenty feet up in an acacia tree. Her knees were badly torn by the thorns. It took two hours to get her down with the aid of block and tackle. One man had climbed up a slim, tall sapling. It bent right over and he was hanging upside down with his head almost to the ground. It was a great ice breaker, though. That night around the campfire, all formalities were forgotten and they were on first name terms.

Travelling along later, there was some discussion about climbing a high fence. I said ' I couldn't climb that.' My companion replied: 'You could if there was a buffalo after you.'

The trip had been full of action so far but I was still no nearer to skiing. A flight from Durban down to East London got me a little closer. Passengers were chewing biltong from bags, just as they would potato crisps.

Early next morning, in the pitch dark, with no stars to see by, I could hear breakers hissing from an inky sea onto the sand as we drove up to the airstrip. A watchman greeted us, well wrapped in an Army greatcoat. Rhodes, our destination, would have been a three hundred mile drive away. So a twin-engined plane, a two hundred and sixty horse power Beachcraft Baron, had been chartered to take me north to Elliot. The flight would be followed by a drive of only sixty miles.

We were so early that the waiting pilot told us that the tower would not be opened until six thirty. But we got on board, the guide first, who sat in the back. I followed Andy, the pilot, into the front. Eventually we took off, the long road journey to Elliott reduced to a flight of a hundred and fifty miles. I was surprised by the pilot's route instructions, a small piece of paper on his lap with pencilled directions. Still in cloud at two thousand feet, we crossed the River Buffalo. After ten minutes, it cleared a bit and there was a little ridge of snow in the distance. Then we were in thick cloud again. I had not realised until then that clear conditions were vital for our spotting the airstrip and the success of the expedition. The range of the 'plane was one thousand and two hundred miles or four and a half hours. So we could not hang about. We three started peering for gaps in the cloud hoping to see any habitation. Then we spotted the town of Elliott below, white painted stones spelling out its name. It was a Sunday so we had to fly across the town with its fifteen hundred inhabitants a couple of times so that our driver, Lionel, could come and meet us. At that moment four Egyptian geese flew by, an unusual sight. We buzzed Lionel who jumped into his car and came and met us. We were in a farming area with a little light industry. The drive to Rhodes would take about an hour and a half, then there would be about half an hour on a rough track to the slopes. But that final leg would be in a four-wheel drive vehicle.

Off we set for Rhodes, through Barkly Pass, near to

Barkly East, both named after Sir Henry Barkly, governor of the Cape in 1874.

The road climbed to five thousand five hundred feet, deep into the surrounding mountains of seven thousand feet. There were eagles, beige /black pigs and tiny lambs curled up in the early morning sunshine. The countryside was like parts of Aberdeenshire but more rugged and without heather. The rocks were of amazing formations and colour. The willows were in a haze of early spring leaves, a springbok leapt by, there were Angora goats and guinea fowl. A road sign said:

'Bright drivers dim

Dim drivers don't.'

The pilot by then was feeling carsick so we rearranged the seating arrangements.

We finally bowled up to the hotel in Rhodes where eager skiers were already waiting in a Landrover. All roads lead to Rhodes on the rare ski days. I joined the others and off we went. The vehicle was packed tight with men, girls, babies and equipment. There was a great feeling of excitement, a bottle of rum was passed around merrily, but I passed it by. This was mainly because I did not relish having my front teeth knocked out by the bottle on the extremely bumpy ride.

The road was precipitous with a little river flowing by. It was real 'roof of Africa' stuff as we climbed. Eventually we were on sheer laterite on a tortuous track. But everyone laughed and shouted and the babies cooed or wailed and there was a general hubbub and feeling of anticipation. Then the road surface changed to a rich black and larks zipped along beside us. In half an hour we had climbed three thousand feet and had reached nine thousand.

The Lesotho border was on the horizon. Cattle rustlers there make their illicit operations easier by wrapping petrol soaked cloths around stones. Set alight, the stones are rolled down the hills and thus over the border. This burns the grass and the cattle graze in a smaller area and the rustlers move in and scoop the pot.

There was snow at the road side and it all looked hopeful. We were making for Ben McDhui, the highest point in the Cape, named by a homesick Scottish surveyor. Skiing is possible for only about nine weekends in a season so we were in luck. A tractor winch ran for about half a mile. The set up was a bit like Chacaltaya in Bolivia. But they did have a piste basher to distribute the snow when it fell.

The operation was planned by four enthusiasts, a doctor, a dentist, a pharmacist and a lawyer. An expert had come from USA to evaluate the feasibility of snow-making and of teaching beginners. At first it was hoped that there could be skiing every winter's day and that, by advertising, a flourishing business would result. But there was too much wind, the temperatures were too high and there was an inadequate water supply so the snow-making idea was a non-starter. Therefore it was not possible to run the skiing as a commercial concern.

The enthusiasts had bought fifty pairs of skis, poles and boots some time before and the rest relies upon Nature. The land is leased from a local farmer and the only run is fairly short. Ironically, more snow falls in Rhodes than on the mountain and the temperature in Rhodes is generally colder too, but the town is on the flat.

There was not a great deal of snow on that day but there was just sufficient to ski a short way and to be able to write about it. The ground without snow was rough. We all had a good time and a tasty picnic. I have always been fortunate in that way, just reaching my quest by the skin of my teeth.

The drive back to Rhodes was even more matey than the outward trip, the depleted bottle of rum still being passed from mouth to mouth. I expected it to be accidentally poured down the back of my neck at any moment with all the lurching of the road. It was getting dark by the time we got back to Rhodes. There was a new moon, golden and slung on its back like a Christmas decoration. There was no mains electricity and water had to be brought from some distance away. We made for the bar, all nationalities, Australian, Canadian and French. They were mostly young and we congratulated ourselves on our amazing feats on the slope.

There was great camaraderie in the dim light of the bar with its wide, polished floor boards. At one point there was a great noise as the leg of a bar stool crashed through a giant crack in the timber floor. Eventually the small children were carried off to bed. I sat on a wooden settle covered with a springbok skin. Soon a sleepy black labrador came and sat beside me and we surveyed the scene companionably. The bar was a great jumble of hundreds and hundreds of bottles. There was an ancient Underwood typewriter, an equally ancient National cash register made in Dayton Ohio. Surmounting the bar were the mounted horns of an ox which had dropped down dead outside the hotel after many years of hauling supplies up there.

A lot of Africaans was spoken. The culmination was when the men sang to me a favourite Africaans song of mine, 'Back in the Old Transvaal.' I recorded it on my little machine. It was one of those magic moments.

When I eventually went off to bed, I was given two hot water bottles, a paraffin lamp, candles and matches. The room had a painted, pressed steel ceiling and the same wide floor boards as the bar. In the morning, it was forty six degrees F in the bedroom. I could then see that there were pressed flower pictures and a bevelled glass mirror on the dressing table. I decided that the hotel would be the ideal setting for a film with a snowed-in scenario.

Next morning there was just time to explore before setting off on the return trip to East London. I was flying back to the UK that night.

Only a few families live permanently in Rhodes. Apart from the hotelier, his wife and son, there was a Post Office, two policemen and their wives and the owner of the general store. I visited the cemetery which bore witness to the hard lives which the pioneers had endured. Inscriptions showed how brief their lives and those of their infants could be. One child from the Biggs family had died aged one year and another even less fortunate was aged only three months and eighteen days.

Then off we set for the journey to Elliott. As soon as we reached the airstrip Andy, the pilot, with some alarm said: 'They've turned the propellers.' Apparently, following riots in Soweto, seven dead bodies had been flown into Elliott from Johannesburg after we left, on their way to burial in their Transkei homeland. Andy then crouched down and started inspecting around and under the 'plane. I too crouched down and had a look. When I asked him what I was meant to be looking for he replied 'Limpet bombs.'

I wondered what my mother would think had she known that I was crawling around under an aeroplane looking for limpet bombs. Happily, nothing was found and we went on our way.

With far better visibility than the preceding day, I had a grandstand view of a great amphitheatre of deep rifts, winding rivers and valleys. The pilot said that it was difficult to slow the 'plane down: 'It just shoots along.' Soon we could see a Boeing ahead which had just taken off from Capetown. Magic. The flight took just forty five minutes and Rhodes was a distant dream.

Fittingly the plane home that night to the UK was called 'Drakensberg.'

Church of the Slaves, Brazil

Chapter Eight

'A painted ship upon a painted ocean.'
Coleridge.

Soon I was flying down to Rio and on to Antarctica, where another encounter would change my life.

When I told Barry Norman, the film critic, that I was going down to Antarctica via Rio and staying at the Copacabana Palace, he said that the hotel had been the setting for 'Flying Down to Rio.' Fred Astaire and Ginger Rogers had danced down the staircase at that hotel. He added that I must get my photo taken there. For one awful moment, I thought that he meant the shot where the girls wing-walk on a bi-plane whilst flying the length of Copacabana beach. On arrival, I mentioned a possible photograph. Before you could turn around, the hotel had produced a photographer and an accomplished Latin American dancer. The staircase had existed only in Hollywood and the scene was filmed there. So the photographs were taken outside, the expert clasping me in a Latin embrace to the surprise of journalist colleagues.

Disconcertingly, a light rain had been falling when we landed, reminding me of the song 'What do you do on a rainy night in Rio?' The answer is that we were taken inland to the hillside town of Ouro Preto, to the oldest opera house in Brazil. All was scented with balsam and lantana.

We covered the sights, marvelled at abseilers on Sugar Loaf and took the tramride across the viaduct to Santa Teresa, Rio's oldest suburb. We ate slivers of beef with beans and rice and casserole of goat and chicken with crisp yam 'chips.'

Then it was off south on a bus to Parati. In a wooden schooner with netting outriggers we were soon enjoying an island picnic. After that we found ourselves stomping along the cobbled street behind a tambourine player in a small procession to the Church of the Slaves which had large wooden doors, painted in turquoise and gold. They swung open to reveal elegant chandeliers and an interior of white and gold hung with blue banners and decorated with Arum lilies. There was time for a shot of Caipirinha, a mixture of lime and goodness knows what. It went down, as the saying goes 'like fixed bayonets.'

Antarctica drew closer with a flight down to Buenos Aires to pick up the ship. Ramshackle lorries, old Chevrolet kitcars and rusty green Jeeps tooted alongside sleek new Mercedes with smoked glass windows. No crash helmets were worn by motor cyclists. Buenos Aires lived up to its name, Good Air: there was no sign of smog or any other pollutant. Prominent was a war memorial for the Argentinian soldiers lost in the Falkland war, La Islas Malvinas.

On a city tour we passed the Main Square. Every Thursday mothers gather to remember their missing children. The blue domes of the Russian Orthodox church, a gift from the Czar, shone in the sunshine.

Our ship was waiting in the River Plate, the spot where the Graf Spee was sunk outside the harbour. On a subsequent cruise some years later, I mentioned the Battle of the River Plate and showed a slide of the harbour in one of my talks. Afterwards, a passenger rushed up to me. She was so delighted: her late father was at the battle and she had never before heard anyone refer to it. Such incidents make all the careful preparation for talks worthwhile.

There was a delay in sailing. The ship's ornithologist took us on an unorthodox 'twitchers' tour which included the one-up-manship of bird watching. A direct descendant of the Pilgrim Fathers, he had several ideas for success when sharing a telescope on a tripod with competitors. He gave tongue-in-cheek ways of staying leader of the pack: as you leave the telescope, unobtrusively move it or readjust the focus knob; if you watch for three or four minutes, the much sought after bird will with any luck fly away before the next person can spot it and lastly, never name the birds that are coming towards you. Despite all this, he showed us a whitefaced ibis, whistling herons, great kiskade, an eared dove, black necked swans, monk paraqueets, white tufted grebes, moorhens, humming birds and a southern lapwing. Dragonflies darted about amongst an abundance of wildlife. There was dark convolvulus tangling about in the acacia trees. Uraguay was only fifty minutes away by hydrofoil.

Eventually we set sail on a pearly evening. I was impressed by the specialist lecturers on board. Little did I know that, within a few years, I too would be one of their number but I would always prefer to describe myself as just a speaker, having no particular expertise. My role now is to encourage others. I always think of the lecturer who asked his audience if everyone could hear. A man called out: 'Yes, I can hear, but I am very happy to swap with someone who can't.'

The passengers were a mix from all walks of life. American voices dominated, each relating accounts of more and more exotic travels.

Twenty-four twitchers from Bristol kept vigil around the clock which proved very useful. In just the short time in which we were in Buenos Aires waiting to embark they told me that they had also seen parrots, a lily trotter, silver teal, herons and white winged coots.

Our route was to take us down the coast of South America and on to the Falklands. From there we would spend a week in Antarctica going ashore wherever possible. Then we would sail back to Tierra del Fuego and thence up to Punta Arenas in Chile before flying home via Paris.

The first few days were sunny and semi-tropical. We were all issued with scarlet Parkas which we would be required to wear whenever we went ashore in colder conditions. All the full length mink coats went back into the cabins until we reached Chile.

As we travelled south to the Falklands we were well briefed about the wildlife. The world's premier site of Rock Hopper penguins, the islands are also home to Jackass and Macaroni penguins. We learnt that the countryside is called Campo, from the Spanish meaning living in camp. The Falklands are the same distance from the south pole as London is from the North Pole which came as a surprise.

The days passed pleasantly; most meals were eaten on deck, the swimming pool was popular as we were gradually being prepared for the great adventure. As the voyage reached cooler climes and we were identically dressed in the red Parkas, it was interesting how all the talk about other destinations and achievements slowly petered out, the bravado evaporating. Captains of industry queued up after lectures to be given, perhaps, a small piece of paper with a little sketch of a bird on it.

The most notable passenger was the grandaughter of Robert Falcon Scott of the Antarctic. There were fitness fanatics who strode around the main deck resplendent in skin tight Lycra with head phones pumping out suitable music.

Soon we passed a dilapidated-looking Japanese fishing boat. I was surprised to hear that the Falklanders themselves do not do much fishing, the rights are sold off to various nations. I overheard an American say to her companion 'I don't need to go ashore at the Falklands, we have Sea World in San Diego. I've only come for the ambience.' Another, newly briefed in defining location by the 'clockface' method, called out 'There's a bird at five p.m.' I have no doubt that I put my foot in it several times too.

As we approached the Falklands I could see the outlines of the hills which had become so familiar from TV news during the war there. On the horizon was Mount Harriet, at 3250 feet the highest point and Mount Tumbledown, its cosy name belying its gruesome recent history. We were told that the nights of 13th and 14th June 1982 were significant in the war. The Scots Guards led a diversionary raid for which everyone was mustered including the cooks. Five hundred Scots Guards formed the main force, making a classic military advance. Thanks to the diversion, they won the battle with only about ten minutes to spare before daylight. I had always heard that, logistically, the Falkland War was a close run thing but I had not realised that it was as close as that.

Near to Stanley harbour was H.M.S. Jhelum, the last surviving three masted barque, a British wooden ship, an East Indiaman. The houses looked flimsy and most, including Government House and the Cathedral, were roofed with corrugated iron. Fences also consisted mainly of corrugated iron sheets just jabbed on end into the soil. But there were lovely flowers, lots of lupins, veronicas, elderflowers, mesembrianthemum, fuchsias and irises. The Upland Goose Hotel was where Max Hastings entered as the first civilian into Stanley when fighting stopped. He writes a great account in his book 'Going to the Wars.' The mother of a friend asked me for tea which was an insight into life on the islands. She remembered when the first Argentinian soldier appeared at her front door, accompanied by a large dog. He was ultra polite and not threatening. She had remained in her house throughout the war. Her son, now an Oxford don, went to school in South America, as do many children from the Falklands.

A short bus tour showed fenced mine fields, peat, rock outcrops and a quarry. There were plump horses; cattle and sheep were penned in stone corralls waiting to be driven down into Stanley by gauchos who came from the River Plate area. There were many less sheep than I had expected.

I had hoped to visit the grave of Col. H. Jones VC but there was no time. But I did find the bronze plaque with the names of all the British troops who were killed and also a dramatic bas-relief. Even though it was ten years since the end of the war, everyone I met mentioned the seventy-two days of conflict.

The land any distance from Stanley was still stiff with land mines. There were skull and cross bone signs along the roadsides, giving constant reminders and warnings.

I visited the only shop, the Pink Shop, painted green. I bought a tape of Kelpers' music which includes a song about the Great White Whale, the name given to Canberra during the conflict.

A woman of eighty seven was on the cruise because she wanted to see what she had missed sixty years previously. Her late husband had been employed in Customs; he had refused a posting to the Falklands as they had a three month old baby. So she was jubilant at having reached her goal.

During the night the ship sailed around to West Point and anchored in deep water. By the time that I reached the deck in the morning, some of the landing craft had been lowered and their drivers were putting them through their paces. Zodiacs, they were sturdy inflatables with thirty horse power Mariner outboard engines. Driving them is a skilled job, as they can easily flip over when not well laden. One of the drivers wore size fourteen waders so I felt almost dainty by comparison. He was huge and joked that he had given up a promising career as a Sumo wrestler in order to come on the trip.

The sea was calm, the whole scene tranquil. Penguins sunned themselves on distant rocks then frolicked by, darting into the water and emerging some distance away. It was sixty degrees F and practically windless.

We all donned our distinctive Parkas and were taken ashore in relays. Rock alyssum, clover and daisies bloomed in the fields. Tea was provided at a farmhouse in a garden smothered in English flowers. The jam was made from the berries of the little plant, the diddle dee. Upland geese, after whom the hotel is named, like to feed on the berries.

There were black browed albatross, pippits and yet more penguins, more densely feathered than any other bird and with a life span of twenty-five to thirty years. Gentoo penguins ran up and down the slopes and porpoises swam in the clear waters.

Then it was off to a penguin rookery. We had been told not to go closer than fifteen feet to the birds. But nobody had told the penguins so they waddled up to us to investigate. Halfway through the trip a pathologist from Nashville said 'I'm kinda burnt out on penguins,' and who could blame him?

As we sailed that evening, giant petrels were bobbing in our wake, imperial cormorants swooped overhead and there were two fur seals lying on a rock.

A sudden blast of icy wind hit us as we went through the narrows, a foretaste of things to come. About a thousand pairs of black browed albatross viewed us from their nests on the cliffs. A killer storm was predicted.

As soon as I put my foot out of the bunk next morning, the wretched feeling of sea sickness hit me, bringing back memories of those pre-war and WW2 Atlantic voyages. A few pills soon put things right.

The Southern Ocean is the only one which circles the globe, flowing past the southernmost tips of the Pacific, Atlantic and Indian Oceans. We were about to enter Drake's Passage: Francis Drake had passed this way in 1578 and was knighted soon afterwards. In the days of sailing ships, it took seventy five days to round the Horn from East to West. Once you had made the trip, you were permitted to sit with a foot on the table in the mess. If you rounded The Horn twice you were entitled to put both feet on the table. As the warmer waters of the South Atlantic pass over the cold Antarctic water, the seas can be the roughest in the world.

In preparation for these rough seas we had been instructed that, if we had to jump into the water, we should hold our noses and cross both arms and legs. Normal rather bulky life jackets were provided. For our trips ashore, we were issued with slimline horse-shoe shaped ones which would inflate automatically when we hit the water.

We crossed Drake's Passage in brilliant sunshine, just a slight swell on the sea.

A giant wandering albatross with an eleven foot wingspan was following the ship, always circling the earth clockwise. Most of the birds which we saw would have been out of sight of land for from three to five years; the albatross had probably not seen land for six years. Generally, the larger the bird, the longer at sea.

Coleridge's 'Ancient Mariner' is based on the account of John Davis' journey in 1592 which he sent to the Royal Geographical Society. Lines were apt:

'And ice, mast high came floating by
As green as emerald.
The ice was here, the ice was there
The ice was all around,
It cracked and growled and roared and howled
Like noises in a swound.
At length did cross the Albatross
Through the fog it came.
(With throats unslaked, with black lips baked)
The horned Moon with one bright star
Within the nether tip.
The moving moon went up the sky
And Spring comes slowly up this way.
The frost performs its secret ministry
Unhelped by any wind.'

This matched our experiences, the moon was there and the frost. But there, thankfully, the similarity ended. We enjoyed marvellous food, there was a cabaret every evening and there were certainly no baked lips.

On any such trip, a journalist will be given a double cabin. Otherwise the sharing arrangements were interesting and unorthodox. Mothers shared with sons, male and female friends doubled up. One such reluctant occupant was heard to say to her unexpectedly amorous cabin mate: 'I'd rather have a curry.'

There was virtually a Chinese village right at the base of the ship. They beavered away doing all the washing;

white towels and sheets were changed daily, always smelling as fresh as though they had been dried out of doors. The Chinese chefs sometimes invited fellow crew members to a banquet, a rare honour.

The Bristol Birders were very helpful. Each morning when I went on deck, there they were, having been up all night, eager to tell me which birds had been spotted.

There were the usual ship's activities. As a guest on the ship and also on subsequent cruises I had been told not to participate in any form of gambling, not to visit or be seen in the casino, not to touch even a gaming machine. Paying passengers understandably are upset if anyone not paying a fare scoops the pool.

Calculating the daily mileage was always popular. This reminded me of a Roald Dahl story. A man with financial problems worked out that he would be able to pay off all his creditors if he could win the bet on the ship's run one day. He worked out that the only way in which he could be sure to win was if he could alter the normal day's sailing pattern. One way to do this would be to make the ship slow down and stop for some time. To accomplish this he would have to jump overboard and would need a witness who would raise the alarm.

He went to the stern of the ship one clear day and started to talk to a woman who was standing there. When he was satisfied that he had her full attention, he deliberately climbed the rail of the ship and jumped into the sea. As soon as he had done this, a nurse in uniform appeared and said to the woman 'Come along, Mrs. So and So, it is time for your rest.' The woman made several attempts to convince the nurse that a man had jumped overboard. But the nurse was quite firm with her, saying that she must be tired and needed her rest. The woman was led away by the nurse. The ship carried on at full speed, the man's arm raised beseechingly from the sea before it finally disappeared.

By now the birders were in seventh heaven, seeing many Atlantic petrels, storm petrels, hooded petrels and great shearwaters. We were told that the first person to see a whale should report the sighting to the bridge and would be rewarded with a bottle of champagne. It was expected that the first sighted would be a Fin or Minke which would probably be spouting. It was not long before one was seen.

By now we were really getting going and awoke one day to find ice on the decks. Eating out was forgotten, swim suits were a thing of the past and the real part of the trip began. Then came the first iceberg, looking like a distant lighthouse, its side lit by the low evening sun.

As the voyage continued, the icebergs became more and more spectacular. They took extraordinary shapes, looking perhaps like Windsor Castle or Sydney Opera House, vast blocks of ice of a lovely turquoise colour. The ice cap at the south pole was then up to three miles thick and ninety per cent of the earth's fresh water was locked in it.

Antarctica was apparently verdant one hundred million years ago. Two percent of the continent is ice free and that was the peninsula for which we were heading. We were in the Weddell Sea, named after an historian.

Our anticipated first destination, the circular natural 'harbour' at Deception Island, was considered not safe to enter. Because of its fumaroles, the enclosed waters are warm and it is the only place for pleasant if unorthodox bathing. An American girl was dashed as she had splashed out on a gold lame swim suit to wear when taking such an unusual dip. But the area is volcanic and some activity was threatened. An indication of this was that the penguins had decided to leave.

Our first landing, therefore, was at Hope Bay. This was on the continental mainland of Antarctica, as opposed to other stops which were islands. The captain said that he liked to get the mainland 'in the bag' as early in the trip as possible in case conditions deteriorated later. We visited the abandoned Chilean whaling station with its country's flag still flying. I omitted to ask how often and how it is replaced. I knew from West Africa that a Union Flag flying over a District Officer's house has a short life. There was a monument in the form of a wrecked boat in which two men had over wintered years before.

In order for us to disembark, a floating steel pontoon had been lowered from a hatch which was at a sea level. We went ashore in the Zodiacs, each of which held twelve including the driver. Cooperation and care ensured that every passenger went ashore. All crew members were pressed into service. The cooks and cabaret artists lent willing hands in a chain as the passengers stepped out of the Zodiacs. We had been told to bring high waterproof boots and waterproof trousers.

There were many penguins wherever we went, their droppings, guano, often a foot deep. There was a strong distinctive smell, not too unpleasant and there were no flies.

Reaching the ship again, we stepped onto the iron pontoon and our boots were scrubbed down with a long brush. Our names were ticked off a list and then we were given a choice of coffee or mulled wine.

By then, wearing the red Parkas was beginning to make sense. Whenever we landed, members of the crew would be stationed at each end of the beach; movement beyond them was strongly discouraged. Had anyone strayed and missed the boat back the only way of seeing them would have been by the bright colour. If anyone had been left behind completely, it would have been curtains for them.

Soon after that we landed at Paulet, a volcanic island. As it is usually surrounded by pack ice, normally only ice breakers get there and most cruise ships fail. After the second attempt we found a safe anchorage. The volcano was venting from several fumaroles and the snow melted as it fell. There were cormorants, penguins, a colony of blue eyed shags and Weddell seals on the beach. The remains of stone huts are there where a Swedish captain, Larssen and nineteen men overwintered. Crossing to the island was quite dramatic and brought home just how remote it was. Three hundred and ninety-two people were landed from our ship on that occasion.

Back on board at teatime, the band was playing 'Come Back to Sorrento' as we all tucked into cakes and eclairs, all rapidly intent, it seemed, on building up as many insulating layers of blubber as that of the balleen whale, whose fat layer is half a meter thick.

The great wandering albatross was still tailing us.

Sometimes, as we sailed as close as was safe to the shore, there would be a thunderous noise. This was the ice 'calving', huge chunks falling off and forming ice bergs. The action preceded the sound so one did not always see it happening.

There were ice clad mountains on the horizon, a continuation of the Andes which swirl down into the ocean at the tip of South America and then emerge much further south. The highest point on Antarctica is fourteen thousand feet above sea level.

Going ashore at different places, we saw more and more wildlife. There were Gentoo, Chinstrap and Adele penguins, the latter named after the wife of de Mondville, a French explorer. Emperor penguins are much further south. A nest is made with a little ring of stones in which the usually sole egg hatches in about thirty-four days. The chicks look like little rounded bowling pins. Unattended chicks soon fall prey to South Polar skuas. After about five weeks the parents start to desert their young. There can be roughly five hundred thousand penguins in a colony.

On a boat once going along the coast of Devon I heard a woman say to her companion 'Look, Ethel, penguins.' There was a group of nuns standing in a cove.

It was not so very long since whalers clubbed seals and harpooned whales. Although the whalers now emerge as the bad boys, it was they who explored and mapped Antarctica. The last commercial fur seal 'catch' was on South Georgia in 1907.

Leopard seals lying in the sun on slabs of ice indicated that it was warmer out of the water than in it. Flocks of Antarctic cardinals and snow petrels flew by. For most of the time the air temperature was just above freezing. Although imperceptible to us as we were never ashore long enough for it to become apparent, the tides rose and fell by six feet or so. Somewhere in the depths were all sorts of extraordinary creatures, the sea spider varying in size from a watch face to a pin head, all its organs on its legs. There would have been sponges living under the ice. Had we inadvertently trodden on any mosses or lichen, they would take decades to recover.

Photographers had a field day. This was before digital equipment and I had been told to keep my cameras warm inside my clothes as far as possible so that the batteries would not be affected. I took two cameras in case of mishaps. As it turned out, I hit no snags.

We were told to leave nothing behind in this pristine land. It did seem to be the only place in the world where there was not a shred of litter and we had not been preceded by the graffiti man with his aerosol spray.

Dogs were banished from Antarctica in 1994. Different forms of transport were tried by different people. Sailing from New Zealand, Captain Scott had taken three motorised Vickers tractors to Antarctica. As they were being unloaded, one slipped overboard and could not be recovered. The other two were not a great success. But the remaining one is still encased in the ice, perfectly preserved. Divers have been around and below it. There was hope a few years ago that it could be recovered and restored. But funds ran low and the plans were abandoned. This was disappointing as I had hoped to go and report on the recovery and the following restoration. The tractor still hangs encased in ice, like a fly in amber, at Scott base.

Some scientists believe that there are six hundred and fifty million tons of krill in Antarctic waters, more than the weight of the whole human race put together. The wandering albatross was still with us. There were twenty thousand pairs on Bird Island alone, each with a wing span of twelve feet.

Yankee Harbour became a whaling station in 1820. On a memorable day, I went ashore and met a fellow passenger from Kansas City. He was holding a pair of skis. There followed the most enchanting time. He was magnanimous enough to share his gear with me. The boots were a bit big but who cared, we clomped up a slope in turns and came rattling down, taking lots of photos. Then he looked at me and said 'You know, Norma, you could be the world's first woman to ski on all the continents.' This sounded a bit far fetched but he seemed fairly confident. Alas, I failed to find him in his home town recently.

At the old Argentinian whaling station of Esperanza, the remains of buildings lay rusting and whale skeletons were scattered about. The death knell of whaling and its by-products sounded finally when palm oil production boomed in 1960's, the palms having been planted in Africa during WW2.

Commerce in the form of drilling for oil and minerals did not seem feasible in Antarctica at that time. The energy needed to drill for oil would probably have been uneconomic.

We made for the Le Maire Channel, Iceberg Alley. A vast iceberg which had recently broken loose had been seen passing through the channel three days previously. Had it still been there when we arrived, no ship could have passed. I was on the bridge at this time, whilst the tricky navigation took place. There were five pairs of skilled eyes on the bridge including two ice masters. They were mostly Swedish. All eyes were skinned, as were the eyes of the passengers on the decks below, all talking intently into their video cameras. Also on board was an observer to ensure that the terms of the International treaties were observed. Every eye was ahead as we made our way through the maze of icebergs. Sea ice stretches quite a long way out from these shores, another hazard to be reckoned with. A radio message in an American voice was received from Palmer, another station. It was a beautiful day there too and they had been playing volley ball for a couple of hours.

The main human activity on the continent is for the advancement of science. We were joined by a scientist from the Scott Polar Institute in Cambridge who had been dropped off at one of the stations by a previous ship. He was studying the effects of tourism on Antarctica and also exploring the possibility of some sort of permanent building for tourist ships to visit. There are no indigenous inhabitants of Antarctica but there has been the rare birth, the first around 1980 at Hope Bay. Lars Eric Linblad led the first tourists to visit Antarctica in 1966 and sailed with us too. At that time, about four thousand tourists a year were visiting the Antarctic, on ships such as ours with reinforced bows.

Straight ahead was Anvers Island and beyond loomed the Agamennon, a high mountain range. We edged along, quite gingerly, admiring a dramatic reflection of the ice cliffs on the bright sea.

Paradise Bay was the next port of call where we were taken ashore at Whaleboat Point. This is the site of an abandoned Chilean whaling station, Gonzalo Videla. After twenty-five years of disuse, it had been cleaned up for the imminent arrival of tourists.

From the Bismarck Strait we reached Port Lockroy, built in 1941 by the British to establish ownership of the region. We were soon ankle deep in penguin slime with mounds of whale bones lying about. A crab-eater seal had a bad cut on its face, perhaps from a fight with a leopard seal. We learnt that elephant seals are twenty feet long and weigh three and a half tons. A pup weighs ninety pounds and trebles its weight in the first three weeks. They can outrun a man over forty yards and can almost keep up with a horse. I made a mental note to steer clear of any.

We fell into a pleasant routine, going ashore by day and sailing on to the next destination by night. Half Moon Island was next, the snowy slopes covered in lichen in colours from red to orange to green. The colours of Antarctica had surprised me, not only the lichens but the blue of the icebergs. On the way back to the ship, we had a Zodiac race with another craft in the blazing sunshine, a brilliant blue sky overhead.

Our final stop was down the Fildes Peninsula at twin manned stations, Marsh which is Chilean, and Bellinghausen which is Russian. There was quite a bustle. Philatelists flocked to the rudimentary post office where they were able also to have their passports stamped. There was a bank and an airstrip. The atmosphere was subdued as a man had been killed in a tractor accident the previous day. A passenger on our ship had had a heart attack so he was taken ashore and flown to Punta Arenas. The girl who had brought the gold lame swimsuit wore it under her Parka so the men manning the station were given the treat of a flash of this garment.

Nearby the Russians were jumping on the band wagon of commerce, with little wooden tables on which were displayed Red Army hats with fur ear flaps, watches and a selection of cameras. One of the most useful pieces of equipment which I had taken with me was a monocular which was also made in Russia.

There was great rivalry between the two stations and curling is a popular sport. A tiny shop stocked various blouses and trousers.

An Arctic tern, the highest flier, cruised along above us. There were many incongruities on the trip, the musicians tuning their instruments unconcernedly as enormous icebergs, some looking very like Edinburgh Castle, floated by almost at arms' reach.

The snippets I overheard during the evenings were interesting. One man said to a friend: 'The best thing about this trip is the films.' These were shown nightly in the cinema in the depths of the ship. Another man said: 'If you have nothing good to say about anyone, come sit next to me.' Landing at one spot was abandoned because of the strength of the Katabatic wind which was screaming down off a glacier, gusting at speeds of up to sixty miles an hour. The Captain reminded us that 'Antarctica has teeth, she will bite. So it is necessary to make quick decisions and the right ones too.' Landing for tourists is really only possible around the area near to the Le Maire Channel and we had been fortunate to have gone ashore every day.

The time came to head north again. Crossing the convergence went almost unnoticed and we were soon heading for Tierra del Fuego. On his travels, noticing the smoke from the fires of the local inhabitants, the explorer Magellan had named the area the Land of Fire. We berthed at Ushuaia, the world's southernmost city. The area is encircled by snow capped mountains, the southern peaks of the Andes. There was the bustle of a port familiar from anywhere in the world. Vetch grew at the water's edge, as did lupins and daisies. Even the dandelions looked strangely exotic. There was yellow broom and sweet william as well as Canterbury bells and columbine. There were ski goods in the shops; the museum housed a wooden figurehead from an early ship. A heavy silver helicopter clattered overhead, another reassurance that we were now back in civilisation, in Patagonia. We were bundled into buses and whisked off to a national park and the world's southernmost bar/cafe where we had little cups of coffee and cream-filled buns. There was a pungent aroma of wood smoke from fires which were heating water for baths for campers who were staying there. We walked near to Lake Roca which is fed with fresh water from the glaciers. A lone mongrel dog sunned itself in the patchy scrub grass. An enormous pig idly watched as we drove off.

On board again, we prepared to sail up the Beagle Channel to Punta Arenas in Chile. I had particular interest in the area. My lawyer brother had had a connection with a ship which went aground and was abandoned in the channel some time before. No lives were lost. He flew out to see what was what. With difficulty, he managed to telephone his secretary in Manchester in order to give her the number where he could be contacted. He made a great show of this with her, asking if she was ready to take down the number, had she got a pencil and paper and so on. When she finally said that she was poised to write down all the complicated details, he said to her: 'The telephone number is Punta Arenas One.' A sideline to the sinking was that my brother had given a Roman coin to each member of the crew. Everyone had had to leave the ship hurriedly and there was no time to take any possessions. So if the oceans run dry, Roman coins will be found in the Beagle Chanel and future historians will be dumbfounded that the Romans had travelled so far. The ship is perched on a rock but we passed it in darkness.

The Beagle Channel had graceful waterfalls cascading into the sea. The Romanche Glacier was impressive, a condor wheeling high overhead. By noon, we reached Fjord Garibaldi. Then the rain clouds came and the decks were awash.

Later, in Punta Arenas on a calm, crisp evening, we were given a debriefing. The fur coats came out again, sensible clothes and trousers were packed away.

Chilean pines, otherwise Monkey puzzle trees were there in profusion. Street names had an historic ring, Columbus Avenue, Magellan Street and The Academia of John F. Kennedy. The man who brought independence to Chile, Bernard O'Higgins, is not forgotten. In the cemetery the yews were neatly clipped and flowers bloomed. In an adjacent field was a unique collection of ancient steam engines, rusting away for lack of funds to house and restore them.

I knew that I had one last thing to do. I had to kiss the big toe of the Indian on the bronze statue of Magellan in the main square. I walked to the spot and was dismayed to find that the statue was enveloped in scaffolding. By then I was wearing a skirt. This was a bit of a problem. But it was no time to be deterred. So, when no one seemed to be about, I hitched up my skirt, climbed the railings and the lower scaffolding and kissed the toe which was already gleaming from previous attentions. Thus my future wellbeing was assured.

By the time that we flew from Chile back to Paris and then to the UK, my mind was already ablaze with plans for the next venture, to ski in Australia.

Raffles, Singapore

Chapter Nine

'The Far Country.'

After the encounter on the beach in Antarctica, on my
return home I set about discovering if I really could be
the world's first woman to ski every continent.

If I did complete the 'bag' it would not of course equal
the tremendous feats of those who had gone before.
After all, anyone with enough money could buy a ticket
to anywhere. I had been to all these exciting places at
no expense. I had been paid, modestly, for my published
articles but then that was the nature of my new career. But
the Guinness record would make quite a useful handle for
my work. Purists will say that there are five continents,
counting north and south America as one and ignoring
Antarctica altogether. Nowadays we more often say that
there are seven.

Guinness confirmed that I could indeed be the first
woman. There are many more records than there is
space in the book as thousands of people hold thousands
of records. Most records never make it into print. I was
fortunate that mine was published in the 1996 edition of
the book.

There was no time to lose. I needed to go south in our summer time. By then placing travel pieces was becoming more difficult. It was all a matter of trust between writer and publisher, prospective hosts and airline. Things change very quickly in the newspaper world. Overnight, a helpful editor is replaced by a stranger. A new editor will have tried and tested writers whose work is preferred.

This was the only time when I decided that I should plough back a little of my small profits and buy an air ticket to Australia. I was given an upgrade which was a big plus on such a long journey. The fare included two nights in Singapore.

It was hot and steamy when we landed there. The majestically wide road from the airport had a central barrier of plants and trees in containers. These could be removed and the road used as a runway in a time of crisis. Raffles Hotel was just across the road from my hotel so I went there the next day.

After reading Agriculture at Aberdeen, an uncle of mine went to Sumatra as a rubber planter before WW1. His local leave was usually spent at Raffles and there were many stories of wild parties there. In 1902 a tiger appeared under the billiard table. A friend of his called Phillips shot it with a Lee Enfield still wearing his pyjamas. Many Sumatran tigers were man-eaters, attacking and killing villagers. One such was shot by my uncle with a Mauser. Photographs show him in pith helmet and tropical 'ducks', the tiger draped over a bamboo pole which is held by two Sumatrans. Villagers stand and admire it. My uncle shipped it home to a taxidermist in Dundee. Its head was stuffed, the mouth lined with a pink substance, the teeth standing out in stark contrast. The body was left flat, backed with brown felt with hooks for hanging.

Throughout my childhood, this fearsome object hung teeth downwards above the staircase of my paternal grandmother's house. It was a terrifying sight; any trip upstairs entailed dodging under the tiger and running for my life. Eventually, the house was sold.

The hall of my brother's house in Cheshire was deemed a suitable spot for the tiger. There it hung for some years until his daughter became a vegetarian. My brother then bundled it up and thrust it at me to find its next home.

I took the tiger back to Scotland. The only place for it in my fully packed car was on the ledge under the back window. Amused lorry drivers hooted and tooted throughout the journey as they passed the lolling tiger, grimacing at them through the glass. It lay, shunned, in the garden shed for some time, giving me a huge fright whenever I came upon it unexpectedly.

Some years later, I read that a tigerskin had realised some thousands of pounds at an auction in Norfolk. I decided that it was time to find a new home for the gruesome family heirloom.

Having on that occasion gone north by train, I had to leave most of my belongings behind in order for there to be room in my suitcase for the tiger. During the journey I reflected that it is just as well that Scotland has not attained full devolution. A suitcase full of tiger might have caused some problems with customs at the border.

I spent a great day at Raffles, starting with 'Breakfast with the Birds', the cafe festooned with bird cages full of singing occupants. A little orchestra with an repertoire evocative of the 1920's played on a balcony and the shops sold souvenirs. The old long bar has been reconstructed, those in the know throwing peanut shells on the floor as has always been the custom.

Arriving in Australia, it felt worryingly that Spring was on the way. The camellias were already fading, the lantana was in crisp minty bloom, the plane trees on Collins Street in Melbourne were bursting into leaf. Clearance sales of winter goods included kangaroo skin steering-wheel covers. Snow seemed unlikely. Then in a sports shop window, a poster read: 'Best snow for twenty years.' That was more like it – what a relief.

During an interview, the local newspaper seemed most interested that I had skied in Europe. I suppose that it sounds exotic to Australians.

Next day it was time to take a bus up to the mountains. There were only seven of us in a luxuriously fitted vehicle, taking the four hour ride to Mansfield. We were eventually to reach Mount Buller. We were making for the Great Dividing Ridge, through the Australian Alps. The driver gave us a lecture before we started, telling us not to put our feet on the seats and generally to behave ourselves.

The dew was still on the golf courses as we sped out of Melbourne. Little trees in white and pink blossom heralded Spring and everywhere there were eucalyptus. The wattle trees were in yellow fluffy bloom and the Yarra Valley and its vineyards lay ahead.

After the Croydon North Shopping Plaza, hills appeared blue in the distance, the valleys filled with mist. A roadside sign said 'WAKE UP: Drowsy Drivers Die.'

From the bus video, I gleaned that more than a million Australians ski each year, mostly at weekends. By now we were in the shire of Alexandra with its clumps of small daffodils. A garage offered snow chains, a hopeful sign. White cockatoos swooped. A hunt was in progress. Foxes, having been introduced, had by then become a pest. Lake Eildon, wide and tranquil, slipped by.

Soon we were in Nevile Shute land, the setting for 'The Far Country.' A brief stop at Mansfield gave us time to visit Buckley's Chance café. Hanging on the wall was the poem 'The Man from Snowy River' written by Banjo Paterson, the composer of 'Waltzing Matilda.' Skiers were congregating from all areas to make the final leg of the journey.

'Chains must be carried at all times' proclaimed the signs. Still, snow and ice seemed unlikely. On we went, through Merrijig and Arlberg. Finally, at the head of a valley, came Buller. We went through the resort pay gates and the snow began to fall with a vengeance. The attendants were muffled up in 'Drisabone' coats and wide brimmed hats. The road cork-screwed on and up, a sheer drop to the left, the eucalyptus trees coated with snow. Cars were stopping in chain-fitting bays. There were banks of snow at the roadside and a real blizzard had begun. The conditions became little short of atrocious. But the road management was efficient and the traffic kept flowing. Four wheel drive was vital and there was much frantic shovelling in the car parks.

When we got out in the heart of Mount Buller, the snow pitted into our faces like icy knives in a true white-out, the temperature well below freezing.

Nevertheless, the ski lifts were running and there was lots of activity. There was a hint of Scottish style skiing, real survival stuff, no poseurs or fancy ski suits.

The atmosphere in the Abominable Snowman Restaurant was authentically warm and steamy, gluhwein fumes blending with the wood smoke. A gale howled outside the misted windows and the snow flew past horizontally. Everywhere was the pungent scent of eucalyptus. In terms of uplift and popularity Mount Buller is the largest resort in the southern hemisphere.

Next day, there were tremendous views of peak after peak. I donned skis and explored the mountain. There was one vital difference from any skiing which I had experienced before. The restaurants and the infrastructure were at the top of the mountain. The runs fanned out downwards and each ended with a four seater

Doppelmayer lift. If you kept heading down, it would be a thousand miles to Sidney through a forest of gum trees.

Staying in a private house, the night had been slightly hair-raising. There was no light switch near to the bed, the nearest being over by the door. The bedroom door did not have a serviceable handle. Two Alsatians viewed my progress to the bathroom with growling suspicion. When I braved my way past them, it was to spot a frisky scorpion with its tail waving threateningly aloft. I did not discover until next morning that Australian scorpions are not poisonous. African ones most certainly are. The first that I knew of this was when, one steamy Nigerian night, a man in a nearby compound was bitten. His cries of agony were terrible to hear. One always had to be vigilant as these creatures will curl up anywhere warm. So, in the morning, it was prudent to tap one's shoes to make sure that they were not harbouring such an unwelcome occupant. Even in the UK the habit died hard. Helping my father in a greenhouse one day, I tapped each flower pot before handling it. He asked what I was doing and laughed heartily when I explained. He and my mother were keen gardeners and most of the flowers were grown from seed. I can see him now, using eyebrow tweezers to repot seedlings into larger containers.

As we headed back to Melbourne next day, there were red parrots in the blackberry bushes, the kangaroos bounding through the fields, jumping amazingly high from a standing start.

The flight home involved some hours in Singapore airport, with its orchid displays. Having exhausted the various delights there I made for the Business class lounge and dozed off on a deep sofa. When I woke up, one of the attendants had draped a blanket over me. I felt like an overgrown babe in the woods.

As soon as I arrived home I again contacted Guinness. I sent photographs of Antarctic skiing, their authenticity enhanced by penguins and an iceberg in the background. I also sent press cuttings of my articles. This satisfied the rules and I was sent a certificate and so the entry was published.

Soon it was time to 'slip the surly bonds of earth' again.

Memorable birthdays and press trips continued. On my first skiing press trip to New Mexico I was sixty-four. So of course the Beatles line kept running through my head 'Will you Still Feed Me?' The start from Gatwick was early and things were quite merry by the time that we took off. We had a jolly flight before changing planes in Dallas. There was a modest celebration on the ground and then a fresh outburst when we got onto the next 'plane. Touching down in Albuquerque, with the time seven hours behind the UK, the day had hardly begun. The head of the ski resort threw a party for us at his house. Entertaining is generally done at various restaurants or hotels on these occasions. So it was unusual to go to his house. It was the longest birthday ever.

Skiing next day was courtesy of our previous night's host. At lunchtime, we were invited to help ourselves from the self service restaurant. The resort was high and I was not feeling particularly hungry. Despite strenuous skiing, I am never very hungry at lunchtime. My moderate choice was a bottle of water, a cup of soup, a roll, some yogurt and a muffin which was wrapped in cling film. When I sat at the table I realised that even this amount was too much. I felt embarrassed to have taken more than I could eat. So I decided that I would take the muffin back to the hotel for tea. Unzipping my jacket, I put the muffin inside. Nobody saw this manoeuvre. Our host from the previous evening then came and sat beside me and put his tray of food on the table. He went off to get something else. After he had gone I looked down and there on the ground was a muffin. Horrors, my muffin must have fallen out. So I picked it up, again unzipped my jacket and put the muffin inside. I breathed a sigh of relief. Our host returned, sat down and began to eat his lunch. He then said 'I have a problem, I had a muffin.' Well now, what a dilemma. It seemed the muffin in my jacket had now been joined by a second one. The question is, what would you have done? I have often told this embarrassing tale. Most people have said that they would have denied all knowledge of the second muffin. When I told my son about it, he said: 'Mum, you didn't tell him, did you?' But, yes, I did. I undid the zip yet again and produced a muffin. I really have no idea what I said to that man, nor what sort of explanation I gave. I could see that he thought that I must be a funny sort of journalist. His alarmed line of thought was that I had been a guest in his house the previous evening and maybe he had better head home and count the silver. Was my face red? When we parted he called after me: 'If you ever need a muffin, Norma…'

At a farewell dinner a few days later the PR people said that they hoped that they would see us all again in New Mexico. When I explained why I might be the exception, they all fell about laughing.

But I have been back, several times. The most memorable was when I went out one October to the annual balloon fiesta, the world's biggest. The event has been held in Albuquerque for over twenty years so they really know what they are doing.

At five in the morning on the day of the flight, we set off for the large area set aside for the event.

Gurus formed the dawn patrol, taking to the skies first to ensure that conditions were safe for the events to go ahead. Launchings are abandoned if the wind is over seven miles an hour. Balloons floated aloft, wonderfully colourful, lit by the occasional puff of propane generated energy. Conditions were favourable so preparations began. I was going up in a mass ascent of eight hundred balloons, taking off within seconds of each other.

Things have come a long way since the Montgolfier brothers noticed that burning paper at their father's factory floated skywards. They thought that the smoke rather than the heat caused this. They soon made their own enchantingly decorated paper balloons and took to the skies. Fuelled by bonfires of noxious farm waste, many of those early balloons burned and crashed. The brothers would no doubt be surprised that two hundred years on, their efforts have spawned such a popular pursuit.

Although the envelopes are now made of polyester and nylon, the wicker baskets remain almost unchanged and are ideal for the purpose. They are woven from giant willow, which looks and behaves like bamboo. Weighing an average of two hundred and eighty pounds, the envelope is unrolled on the ground and initially inflated by a fan.

It was a seething mass of activity, balloons being unloaded from trucks in all directions. I had been introduced to Doug and his wife by now, both pilots and to their balloon, Sky Dancer in which I would travel. Doug was distinctive in a replica of his father's B17 leather jacket and cap from WW2.

It was at this stage of things that I decided that I would make for the row of Portaloos before the great adventure. I was told to be quick. It was all a bit confusing. Fresh from the UK I had not by then figured out if I was a 'Caballeros', the cubicles being thus signposted. It reminded me of the girl visiting the wild west with her boy friend. In a restaurant, she turned to him and said: 'Say, Elmer, am I a heifer or a steer?' Eventually I found the Damo.

By the time that I emerged, a very short while later, the whole scene had changed dramatically. Moments before, the launch site had been an area of pick-up trucks. Now, there was a sea of inflating balloons, all different and none recognisable.

Had I come halfway across the world only to miss the flight? I could see the article slipping metaphorically through my fingers. But all was well. I eventually found Doug.

Even with longer legs than most, I still felt like some gangling primate as I swung into the basket. Four propane cylinders stored at each corner would last for a two hour flight. Five people had to hold the whole contraption down as Doug prepared for take-off. They would watch our progress and race in a truck to be there for our landing.

I had thought that I might be a bit frightened after experiences in single engined 'planes and in the glider but all this was forgotten as we slowly became airborne, waving to some of the two hundred thousand daily visitors.

The ground temperature had been forty-one degrees F, but there could be an upward swing of as much as thirty degrees as the day progressed. Even when we had risen just a short way, it was suddenly warmer. I leant against the suede bound edge of the basket whilst Doug explained to me why that area of New Mexico is ideal for ballooning. The winds are predictable and there is also the unique 'box' phenomenon of opposing winds and currents. This ensures an almost regimented route, moving from one layer of currents in one direction then either rising or falling to catch a current going the other way. In fact, there was a double box on this particular day which enabled us to travel back and forth over the Rio Grande. Doug explained reassuringly that he is always alert for other balloons, above and below. Wind direction is determined by watching smoke, flags, steam from power stations and anything else to give a clue to conditions. He equated his hobby as akin to three dimensional chess. So all the time you have to figure out where the currents are; you might go west in a current that is a hundred feet thick. Then you could drop below, it is always changeable. That morning the cold air had formed a layer which was about four hundred feet deep.

As soon as the sun came up, everything changed again: it was at least fifteen degrees F warmer. Then as the sun rose higher, it set up little currents in different directions.

As we drifted along, I could see that all our friends with whom we had taken off in sequence were still keeping pace with us in the same formation.

The fiesta includes various competitions. Perhaps a pilot will drop a bean bag as close to a marked X target as he can. Another time maybe a key will hang from a thirty foot pole. The lucky winner will swoop down and retrieve the key which might fit a car as a prize. One year, somebody won a house.

The flight was a bit like floating in a bowl of Faberge eggs or children's spinning tops. Some balloons were exotic shapes, the old lady in a shoe with many children attached was the equivalent of fifteen storeys high. A waving Michelin man floated amidst it all, also pigs and cows. Even the Orient Express engine was there complete with sound effects of a siren. There were elephants too and a balloon from BT. Doug said that there were entries from sixteen countries and from forty-one of the American states.

I decided, though, that having had the excitement of take-off, ballooning is a bit limited in its appeal. Direction of flight and speed is determined by the wind, you cannot suddenly decide to drop in on friends, or make any real plans for the trip. I enjoyed it all but after an hour or so,

I felt that I had experienced the extent of the activity. I began to feel quite weary having had little sleep and no breakfast. Then Doug said that it was too windy to land and that we would stay up for another hour or so. I said to myself: 'I know what is going to happen next, I'm going to faint in this nice man's basket.' This was a real possibility. I have not fainted often but I know the signs. The first time that it happened to me was at school. We were singing 'Onward Christian Soldiers' when I hit the deck. Stalwarts carried me out to the sickroom. The whole episode became embarrassing. Bodily functions, particularly female ones, were cloaked in a web of euphemism. The head mistress appeared and asked me if I had my 'Little Visitor.' I had not the faintest idea what she was talking about.

In the balloon basket I took a few deep breathes and averted a faint. As we approached the ground, the basket turned onto its side. Terra firma and all its rubble raced towards me. I then heard Doug shouting to someone on the ground, 'Move the truck! move the truck!' Our own back-up team plus truck were already stationed nearby, ready to help with our landing, as planned. But another truck of enthusiasts, seeing that we were landing rather fast, had raced to the rescue. Their driver in his enthusiasm abandoned his vehicle, hoping to help. But we were speeding towards his truck,which was not a good idea. At first, amidst all this, I thought that I was going to lose my teeth, an awful thought. As we continued to hurtle along, I was getting mouthfuls of grass and grit. I thought that my face was going to get ripped up. I eventually thought that I might lose my entire head. But eventually all was well and we came to a stop. I staggered out of the basket. A bottle of champagne was produced.

After that it was north to El Rancho Encantado where I stayed in a cottage room with a corner fireplace. It was roofed with Ponderosa pines. On many buildings in

New Mexico these project beyond the eaves and make a convenient place on which to hang awnings in the hot weather. Robert Redford's ranch was nearby which added a frisson of excitement. It was real 'Horse Whisperer' country.

The next commission to the state was to write about Route 66 which was completed in 1924. Known as the Mother Road, the route was celebrating its 75th birthday in some style. Originally two thousand four hundred and eighty miles long, it was decommissioned in 1984. Our own British A 66, running into Scotch Corner, doesn't somehow have the same ring. Driving on the right needed a bit of practice The leafy car park at the hotel seemed a suitably safe spot. A white Lincoln stretch limo, nearly thirty feet long, was provided and presented no problems. Its 350 hp engine purred quietly as I gingerly negotiated the corners. I was soon quite at home. When driving on the right, Stirling Moss changes his watch to the other wrist. This is a good tip as it acts as a reminder that things are reversed.

Route 66 runs through the heart of Albuquerque and lots of landmarks remain. The Filling Station Cafe on 3001 Central still has a feel of its original use. Lunch consisted of typical New Mexican food. Earlier, in 66 Diner (which was Sam's 66 Service Station in 1946) also on Central, I downed the thickest, creamiest milk shake ever. So we moved along the route, sampling its delights as we went, finishing up at Nob Hill, the posher part of town, its name probably a corruption of Snob Hill.

In the adobe style hotel, the plate for the door number of each room had a circle on it, followed by a line of dots, which symbolises a journey in progress. On the wall of each room a rug hung over a pole. This is the American Indian's equivalent of a coat hanging in a wardrobe, the garment there in readiness for going out. A ladder is often propped against an adobe building, the poles disproportionately long. This ensures that the wood pierces the sky and brings rain. I went on a hayride one day with Mike, whose father had given him a candy apple red Chevrolet Camero for his graduation when RT66 was at its most popular. As the horses jogged along, pulling the wagon, an eagle suddenly swooped down and carried off a rattlesnake. My fellow occupants asked Mike how they trained the bird to do this! Yet another rattlesnake crossed our path and Mike quickly dispatched it and gave me the rattle.

Riding a mountain bike along a trail down through the cottonwood trees to the Rio Grande was a thrill. That great river, swelled with snow melt from the Rockies, was rolling along down to the distant Gulf of Mexico.

From 1928, Gallup to the west on Route 66 was used as a backdrop for films. Dozens of film stars stayed at its hotel, El Rancho. Not far away, the Continental Divide at 7,268 feet is the spot where waters to the west flow into the Pacific and those to the east flow into the Caribbean and the Atlantic.

The journey there included a stop at the bar at Budville: thirsty country. Coffee is free to anyone eccentric enough to want it. New Mexico's state bird, a roadrunner, straight out of a Disney cartoon and a member of the cuckoo family, zapped across the road in front of us at about twenty mph, with a rather indignant look. Clumps of tumbleweed rolled across the road.

Then it was on to Acoma, featured in the book 'Death Comes for the Archbishop.' Dating from 1150, it is USA's oldest continuously inhabited settlement. Seen from a distance it was like a transplanted Ayers Rock rising out of the vast plain. It is still home to thirty families. The church is sacrosanct – even note-taking seemed inappropriate. The surrounding graveyard was pathetic. In ancient times children were abducted from the settlement by the Spanish, never to return. There are holes in the mud walls of the cemetery so that the returning children could crawl in again. They never did.

Having committed murder, an early priest was thrown over the edge of the settlement to his death. Another priest was treated in the same way. But history has it that his robes must have acted as a parachute. The locals, descending to recover his body, saw only a set of footprints heading into the distance.

Dawson City, Klondike

Chapter Ten

'Were you ever out in the Great Alone,
when the moon was awful clear,
And the icy mountains hemmed you in
with a silence you most could hear?'
Service.

As my late writing career progressed, I met a man from Alaska at the World Travel Market in London. Knowing that I was always looking for something unusual to write about, he said ' Why not come and ski inside the Arctic circle with dogs?' Why not? This was music to my ears and plans were soon made. The ski magazine and The Scotsman newspaper in Edinburgh expressed interest so it was full steam ahead. I had not given a great deal of thought to the meaning of 'skiing with dogs' but I had got hooked on those three words.

A first class plane ticket to Anchorage materialised for a day in May. Arrangements were made through the Alaskan department of tourism. On subsequent working visits to Alaska, I always encountered the same taxi driver at the the airport. Architecturally, Anchorage

171

was a surprise, with almost a touch of the Wild West or some West African town about it. A smattering of large hotels and department stores soon peters out to single-storeyed buildings, looking none too substantial for such an inhospitable climate. But the temperature on my arrival was 45F. For Alaskans, Spring had arrived and they strolled the streets, a girl in a cotton skirt and bare legs, a man in shorts and white linen jacket. I was well wrapped up. A bus had 'Arctic' on its destination board. There was also a sign to remind the driver to check under the seats at the end of the day for stray children. Had they inadvertently been left in the bus overnight in the winter they would have suffered a nasty, cold fate.

We set off in an old Dodge taxi, along Northern Lights Boulevard. A stuffed polar bear, standing on its hind legs in the lobby of the hotel was truly fearsome. Its claws were considerably longer than my fingers. I felt more foreign than I have felt anywhere before. This sounds absurd from someone who spent early formative years in North America. I seemed to have an amazingly alien accent. I asked for a 'raspberry yogurt.' Even after several attempts, my accent was incomprehensible to the waitress. I eventually adopted a more local pronunciation, the waitress' look saying: 'Why didn't you say that in the first place?' The beer-battered halibut which preceded it was wonderful.

The next morning I walked past an Inuit who said 'Lady, you've got a lovely nose,' which was a good if undeserved start. At breakfast, I avoided the reindeer sausage, it smacked too much of Santa.

Then it was time to fly north to Fairbanks, about three hundred miles away.

Checking in, my luggage and I were both weighed. The inflight food consisted of milk and blueberry muffins. It was explained that we could use our seats as flotation devices, unlikely as the flight was entirely overland. At Fairbanks airport, with its stuffed bison and muskox, I transferred to a nine seater, twin-engined Markair Express Piper Navaho. The only passenger, I sat in the co-pilot's seat. As we taxied, the pilot showed me the emergency exit and also told me that the gun, a 44 Magnum Bristol and camping equipment were in the wing. I asked where he would be when I manned the gun but he was silent on that point. One in every fiftyeight Alaskans at that time had a 'plane and a licence to fly. Under Alaskan state law a gun is required to be carried. These small 'planes sometimes come down in wild territory, landing safely. Bears roam freely so a gun could ensure survival. The largest carnivore, the grizzly or brown bear is a big beast.

In 1898, the pilot's grandfather was sixteen. He ran away from Sarejevo and stowed away on a ship to Baltimore. The pilot's father became Territorial Governor of Alaska before it became a state in 1959.

The early settlers were called sourdoughs: a staple of their diet was such a dough. It is leavened bread containing no yeast. On the lines of the ginger beer 'plant' in UK, it lasts for months and was shared around the community.

We crossed the Yukon River, the ice just starting to break up. Tradition had it that, crossing the river, you added to the fluid content. At over nine thousand feet we instead companionably shared a chocolate chip cookie. The temperature outside was 2 F, very cold. The oil pipeline from Prudoe Bay, four feet in diameter, lay below. With seventy one remote gate valves, the flow of oil can be stopped within four minutes so the danger of seepage is negligible. Its walls have rubber bricks which would absorb any shocks from an earthquake.

Around twenty miles south of our goal, we crossed the Arctic circle.

Our destination, Bettles, was part of the DEW (Defence Early Warning) network and was staffed by the Military. The gravel airstrip, measuring 5,200 feet is long enough for a Hercules to land. A posting to Alaska attracts overseas pay, applicable even to Alaskans who are amused to be paid an overseas allowance to live in or near their home towns.

Accessible only by air in the winter and by river in the summer, Bettles, with just a few dozen inhabitants, was rated a second class city. In order to be a first class or home rule city, there must be over four hundred inhabitants. The city then provides public education and also levies certain taxes.

The lodge at Bettles had been opened up early for me. On arrival, the temperature was 22F. I went to see the huskies, which were extraordinarily hardy. Very often snow blocks entry to their individual kennels. Even with temperatures as low as -70F they curl up outside and sleep quite happily. As the lodge is used usually only in summer, there is no electricity and lighting is never needed. We were just weeks from the summer solstice. It was 10th May but still very cold. I slept with my ski hat on.

Next day, the sun was high in the sky by 7am. A breakfast of waffles and maple syrup laid the foundation for a full day ahead. The water had a metallic taste as most of the rivers have iron in them. As I stepped out of the lodge in blazing sunshine, my foot crashed through the crusty snow to knee height. A snowshoe hare gambolled nearby, its furry hind feet keeping it on the surface. Behind the lodge the remains of a moose lay in the snow, the eye sockets empty. It had provided ample meat for two people all winter.

When moose are killed on the roads in towns, needy inhabitants can be put on the 'Moose Kill list' and are given a share of the meat. No freezers are needed in those climes, all that is needed is protection from wolves and other predators. A cache provides this, a tree house out of reach of hungry inquisitors.

The guide, Dave, explained what skiing with dogs entails. The idea is to don narrow cross country skis, harness up dogs and whiz along behind them. Housewives in Fairbanks keep two huskies which pull them to the shops.

Preparing for another flight in my quest to ski with dogs, we loaded four huskies into a Piper Cherokee Six. I had heard of flying doctors but this was ridiculous. This pilot told me that he had once flown fourteen dogs in a Super Cub.

The cargo consisted of a sled, skis and a box of provisions. The idea was that we would fly about a hundred miles north and land on a frozen lake.

The dogs were not too keen on boarding the plane and did not enjoy the journey much. I certainly did as we flew low over forests and lakes with abundant wildlife. Caribou herds bounced along and grizzly bears ambled. There were wolves, foxes, moose and dall sheep peculiar to Alaska. Porcupines hung high in tree branches looking like carelessly discarded Davey Crocket hats. Porcupine are not as innocent as they look. Their quills are like darts and can travel along a victim's blood vessels and reach the heart. We flew over Death Valley and Death Creek, chilling names that stemmed from nothing more sinister than forest fires.

As before, a gun was carried. Dave and Andy the pilot both carried knives. These they described as an insurance policy, rather like carrying a credit card in town. We flew over a mining road, where it was still possible to find gold. Eventually Wild Valley was ahead with its pines, snow and still partly frozen rivers. Then Wild Lake, our proposed landing spot, snaked along in the distance. As we neared,

I was surprised to see a figure standing waiting on the ice. On landing, I was even more surprised to see that it was a very pretty girl. I realised then why we had come to this particular lake and why we were carrying provisions. The guide and the pilot were both, understandably, keen on Caroline.

Late in the season, there was not enough snow on the ground for a safe landing. So we landed on the lake where the ice was about seven feet thick. Had we arrived a few weeks later, we would still have been able to land on the ice. But the edges of the lake would have thawed and we could have fished for our lunch in the clear water. Our catch would have consisted of trout, grayling, pike and Arctic char.

After we had all hugged Caroline, she explained to me what had brought her to that remote spot. Her parents were 'home steaders' and she determined to try her hand at the same solitary life. In order to encourage immigration, the Government would lend a hundred and sixty acres of land to an individual. If they clear the land and build a house, they are eventually given title to the land. This seemed similar to the New Forest in the past where those who had their chimneys smoking within twenty four hours of building their houses could claim ownership. Caroline had arrived the previous summer, had cut down the pine trees herself and built an impressive log cabin.

It was then time to try 'ski joring' ie 'skiing with dogs.' A similar activity takes place in Hungary but that entails 'skiing' behind horses on grass. The dogs were more than enough for me and were delighted to be free, rolling in ecstasy on the ice and chewing its granular surface. Victory, the lead dog and fourteen years old, was clearly still in his prime. Squirt, his most junior colleague justified his name by singling out my boot as one of the few vertical objects for miles around.

I donned the narrow skis. Dave harnessed the dogs and the theory was that they would pull me along. Weighing between forty and sixty pounds, the dogs are lean and light-boned. It was incredibly difficult to get a grip on the icy surface and the whole procedure proved tricky. Andy the pilot tried but said that it was 'glare ice', very smooth and he also fell often. It was slightly easier when the sled was harnessed behind the dogs and the skier went along behind the sled. Even then it was more difficult than it sounds. It was vital not to let any of the dogs loose. A fit young husky loves to run and will go all day without tiring. Had one broken free from its traces, we would never have seen it again.

Still the sun blazed down and off we went to Caroline's nearby cabin. Andy and Dave pulled her along in the sled. Wrapped in furs, she might have been approaching Camelot. Her outside 'privy' consisted of a plank over an outdoor pit some distance from the cabin. She told me that she spent most of her time looking for wood to burn for cooking and heating. She had a solar powered torch and radio which were on the narrow window sill. Her bed was on a shelf at one end. She had heard a movement at her door only that morning but did not open it in case it was a bear. Another girl whom I met later on said that she had shot a twelve foot high brown bear in its face when it tried to attack her. Despite this, it still pursued her at great speed, dropping eventually.

At the end of one of life's unforgettable days, we left Caroline to her solitary life. I asked Andy how she would fare in a medical emergency. He said that she would have a satellite device from which passing Jumbos could pick up any emergency signals. This sounded a bit hit and miss to me: when is an emergency not an emergency?

What if she had terrible toothache? Glad to be back in comparative civilisation I went to a basketball match in the sports hall at Bettles.

The following day it was time to fly back to Fairbanks and to pick up the Alaskan Railroad to Talkeetna. A large rooster of a train, it had a sturdy cow-catcher at the front and a hooter with an eerie wail. Snatches of overheard conversations were similar and yet different from those elsewhere. Two women behind me companionably swapped household hints. One told the other how to make bear stew, beginning 'First get the bear meat out of your freezer.' That's nothing, as I discovered when I bought an Alaskan cookery book. Recipes appear for Deep fried muskrat, Jellied moose nose, Roast mountain goat, Roast bear, Caribou sausages and Moose chilli. The veggie lobby had not yet arrived in those parts.

I was met at Talkeetna and taken to the airstrip. The plan was to fly me up to the base camp of Mount McKinley, named after a President of USA who never visited Alaska. This time I was in a Cessna 185, fitted with skis.

North America's highest peak, Mount McKinley lies in Denali (Great One) National Park. The honeymoon couple with us had picked their code name 'Peaches and Cream.' They were very excited and had planned this climb for a long time. Kahaltna Glacier stretched below for forty five miles. Next came Glacier Valley, four miles across and with 18,000 foot mountains looming on all sides.

We went past 'One Shot Pass.' Looking down a deep crevasse, I suddenly had a horrifying idea of what it would be like if the plane came down and we plunged into the chasm. The stuff of nightmares.

The landing at base camp at 7,000 feet was unusual. In order to stop in time, we landed uphill, heading into the side of the mountain. Conversely, the take off took place downhill, which was just as effective but not so alarming.

Kitted out with cross country skis, I clomped around the base camp. I asked if there were any British climbers and was told that three RAF men were already up the mountain. I noted their names from the Visitors' Book. To my dismay, their names were front page news on my return to the UK as they had all been killed on the mountain.

On my first visit to Alaska, as with everywhere else, I had bought a road map. It was not a lot of use as there are hardly any roads and the rivers are frozen in the harsh winters. I had heard of the Yukon Quest, a husky race from Fairbanks to Dawson City. But the Iditorod husky race sounded even more gruelling. It is held annually to commemorate an heroic relay to the northern town of Nome. In the cold weather of 1925 its inhabitants were threatened with an outbreak of diphtheria which was deadly at that time. Access was impossible. It was decided to organise a relay of husky dogs and their mushers to take the vitally needed serum to Nome. This was achieved, and the population were thus saved. The journey was repeated in 1967 not as a relay but for single mushers racing to Nome itself. Just fifty six miles were covered in the early race.

In 1973 the course was extended and ran from Wasilla, near to Anchorage, to Nome. Although the race takes its name from a township on the original route, on alternate even years the course goes on a more northerly loop. The bond between man and dogs is vital for survival. Competitors rarely have more than two hours' sleep each night. Towards the end of the race, competition is so intense that most mushers have no sleep for the last three days.

Although the distance is roughly 1100 miles, the official length is always given as 1049 miles because Alaska is

USA's forty-ninth state. It is tough going. Mushers start with anything up to twenty dogs. More than that number would be difficult to handle. Contestants must finish with at least five. Everyone concerned is a volunteer. With twenty-four checkpoints to man along the route, vets are kept busy. The volunteer pilots of the Iditarod Air Force ferry supplies and also take any unfit dogs back to base. The event culminates on the second Saturday in March with a banquet for a thousand people, held in the sports hall at Nome. This fixed date allows time for the recipient of the Red Lantern, the slowest racer, to arrive. Copious food for the dinner is flown up from Anchorage. The best role for me seemed to be as a volunteer waitress.

I went out the previous summer to lay plans for the trip. The local hotel and newspaper share a name, the Nome Nugget. The former lacked only Klondike Kate, high kicking down the staircase in black fishnets. I was met by Richard, supremo of Nome's activities, who had many amusing experiences to relate. In the mid-1960's, he was an actor, appearing in pantomime in Cambridge. An American citizen, he was working illegally in the UK. On stage, dressed as a mouse, he heard that the authorities were on his tail. With not a moment to lose and fortunately with a diminutive frame, he escaped through the dressing room window and fled through the streets of Cambridge in the mouse costume. He met my 'plane at Nome, having swapped his furry garb for a bright pink baseball cap. He had had many jobs including tap dancing, singing in New York and selling freezers to Eskimos.

We spent an unforgettable day out in the countryside. At one point, he said 'We'll boogie on to Pilgrim.' The river there was so full of salmon that we could have crossed it by walking on the backs of the gleaming fish. Sharing my love of musicals, our repertoire featured 'If our Friends could See us Now' which we belted out enthusiastically at every opportunity.

Then it was on to the Arctic Circle and Kotzebue on the far north west coast. There was a feel of excitement in the air, people whizzed about on Honda Fourtrax, sturdy four-wheeled buggies; children were out playing and laughing in the sunshine at nearly midnight. The shop seemed never to close. Having seen an advert for a particular make-up on the TV in my room, I went along to the supermarket just after midnight and bought some. Had I not kept the airline eyeshade I would not have been able to sleep. At one in the morning the sun still blazed fiercely through the bedroom's thick curtains having dipped below the horizon for just a few minutes.

The local museum featured a demonstration of Inuit look-out technique. Standing on the ice, about eight people would hold a large dried skin or a blanket. The lightest of them would then be tossed high in the air, turning in a different direction with each toss in order to spot possible game or to see the way home in such featureless territory. Fur clad young people showed various 'games' to while away the long dark winter days. One of these was High-Kick Football, a solo game of one-legged football. Standing on one leg, the player jumps in the air and attempts to kick the ball. Some years later, giving talks on a cruise ship, I tried out this tactic in my cabin before giving a talk. I apologised to the occupants of the cabin below as they surely thought that I would come crashing through their ceiling.

Early Eskimos were ingenious, making drums and windows from the lining of walrus' stomachs, platters from flat moose antlers and sewing 'thread' from the sinews of a caribou's back leg. With this they stitched their skin and fur clothing.

Houses are built on stilt-like springs which keep the foundations above the perma frost, which is only a foot or so down. Otherwise the comparative warmth of the house would melt the perma frost and the house would sink.

Returning to Nome the next winter for the Iditarod, it was difficult to distinguish land from frozen sea as we approached the airport. The only clues were little tufts of tundra grass on the land. Prior to the race, a musher prepares packs of provisions for his dogs and himself. These are taken to each checkpoint. The huskies wear little bootees and these have to be replaced often. How they stay on is a mystery. Reached by an ice road, the race's final checkpoint at Safety was a truly desolate spot.

Whatever time of day or night mushers complete the race, there is always a good welcome. The town's siren sounds as soon as they are spotted. The mayor or deputy and someone from the local paper welcomes every musher to Nome. Looking at the lean huskies as they came in, it was amazing to think that they had run over a thousand miles. They still seemed fresh and ready to keep on running. Beards had become frost rimed in the ferocious cold. The greetings take place under a gnarled oak arch with welcoming banners. I witnessed the first proposal of marriage on the finishing line. The competitor was met and accepted her boy friend's offer and a ring.

The following morning was the day of the banquet. As I trudged through knee-deep snow in the vicious cold, it seemed a pity that Fat Freddie's, Mecca of Nome's cuisine, was not yet open. Breakfast would have to come later.

The setting for the banquet was the large recreation hall, four streets inland. It was well equipped with hanging basketball nets. It buzzed with activities as volunteers assembled tables and chairs. Eager hands taped white paper cloths to the tables and festooned the walls with sponsors' banners. It was to be a self-service occasion and there were several points where diners could collect their food.

Five hundred pounds of prime beef were to be carved by high-hatted chefs at various spotlit tables. Five hundred pounds of giant shrimps were piled into sledges which were first lined with cling film. Every sort of accompaniment was there. Preparations took all day. We were given a short break when we all went back to the hotel, by which time Fat Freddie's was up and running, crammed with ravenous mushers and helpers, most people in loud checked shirts, the food an array of fried fare, all served in a gloriously warm and steamy atmosphere. Revived, we headed back to the hall.

Eventually everyone started arriving. Nearly a thousand people was quite a handful. It was interesting to find what power one has as a waitress, taking food to friends so that they did not have to stand in line and wait. By the time that everyone had finished eating and we had cleared away all the plates, I was feeling a bit weary. I thought longingly of my bed back at the Nome Nugget. But I pulled myself together and decided that I had not come all this way across the world for an early night. We all settled down for the prize-giving and speeches. Each one of the fifty-eight finishers made a speech and was presented with a handsome belt with an impressive buckle. One man remarked 'Never have so few dogs run so far for so little.'

Stories were told of haunted shanties en route. The winner had stayed at the Old Woman cabin and had felt the presence of the Eskimo. One musher, in a low voice, spoke of a different expedition when the ice on Great Slave Lake had cracked and he lost twenty dogs, all drowned in five minutes. There were tales of wolves ranging outside the cabins.

During that year's race, five mushers, one unconscious, were rescued from a tent filled with carbon monoxide. Dr Beth Baker had managed to revive them. A 'Rookie' on her first race, she lost time towards the $50,000 prize but was fittingly presented with the Sportsmanship Award. Frostbite was not uncommon. One man had a broken leg with a plaster to prove it. A hat was passed around for his medical expenses as he was not insured.

As I left, the Aurora Borealis were so bright that they cast shadows.

Soon afterwards, still pursuing unusual skiing, it was time to go 'Dipping through the Tropics by the palm-green shores.' Destinations for my skiing articles became known to me by various means. Flying over Hawaii, a friend was amazed to see a snow-capped peak on the Big Island. Just short of the International Date Line, this Polynesian Island discovered by Captain Cook would seem an unlikely place for skiing. If it were measured from the sea bed, its extinct volcano, 14,000 ft. Mauna Kea (White Mountain) would be the earth's highest mountain, higher than Everest. Because of the exceptionally clear skies, over a dozen observatories were then sited on the summit. Often there is a cape of snow there from January until May and this was what I was after.

Comfortably settled for the trans-Atlantic flight, I thought as always of the Pilgrim fathers. They pitched about on the Mayflower, people dying, a baby being born, rats and disease rife. A passenger nearby was elegant, beautifully dressed and coiffed. She suggested that I come and talk to her. She asked what I was doing and was surprised to hear that I was going to Hawaii to ski. She asked where my last assignment had been. When I said that it had been Alaska, she said that she knew it well, that her husband had had interests there. When I asked if he had been an oil man she said, no, he had had an interest in the theatre in Anchorage. He was Boris Karloff. The rest of the flight flew by with such an intriguing companion.

Honolulu and Pearl Harbour both lie on the island of Oahu. The hotel in Waikiki was right on that famous beach. I spent a night there before heading off to the Big Island. It was exciting, still, to arrive and be handed an envelope addressed to me, c/o Daily Telegraph, London. It contained an updated itinerary from the local tourist board. A twenty minute flight next day took me over to the Big Island. This, the youngest of a group of six main islands, is still growing because of frequent lava flows. Real fire and ice country, several active volcanoes spew and hiss their molten way into the surrounding ocean, very different from Waikiki. The approach to the airport was over a field of black lava.

Moving around the hotel, from reception to the rooms, to the seven restaurants, cinemas, theatres and pools was all by water along manmade canals. The boats were spick and span, manned by crews in pseudo naval attire. The lush palms had been brought from other islands. Over two thousand staff used ten thousand orchids a day for decoration. My room was scattered with these from bedside to bathroom.

The only thought in my mind was reaching Mauna Kea and for there to be enough snow for skiing. I had been told that the main enthusiasts who ran trips to the snows had had a serious road accident and that they could not be contacted.

The hotel's guide-cum-driver had a degree in Leisure Management. Tongue in cheek, he said that he was thinking of topping it with a Doctorate in Extended Sleeping. We set off up the mountain but hit a serious snag on reaching Pohakloa State Park at six thousand feet. We could go no further as flash floods had closed the road ahead. It was the last possible day for me to get to the snow as I was flying back to Waikiki the next evening. The only bright spark was that the warden there had a three legged dog called Tripod.

Disconsolately I returned to the hotel. One can always glean facts and somehow write an article without actually experiencing what you are writing about. But I have always felt that this is dishonest and I have never done it. Walking around the hotel that evening, I saw the most wonderful pearl necklace in the jeweller's. I've always loved pearls and these were irresistible. Many people think that pearls are unlucky. I have never been superstitious about pearls and have had no superstitions at all for the last few years. This is because my son suddenly had to have an emergency brain operation when on holiday in France. On the drive to the airport to be with him, everything which I had ever been so superstitious about happened, lone magpies flew by, black cats ran from the wrong side of the road to the other and so on. In those hours the frailty of human life was brought home to me. He made a complete, trouble-free recovery. From that day I have realised how absurd it is to be superstitious. A brief spell of looking down the barrel of a gun had cured me.

As soon as I had bought the pearls, I had an inspiration. I would after all telephone the company from which someone had had an accident. A bright voice answered immediately. The accident had been a minor one, nobody was hurt, the firm was very much in business and they would be delighted to take me to ski the next day. The road had been repaired by the US army who were on manoeuvres nearby. There would be plenty of time for them to take me to ski and then drop me at the airport for my evening flight back to Waikiki.

Part of our route to the mountain was along the road to Hilo, where most of the island's abundant supply of orchids is grown. Twenty miles 'shy' of Hilo we turned left off the main road and the real business of the day began. In another two hours, we reached Waimea, through rolling ranch lands which rose to four thousand feet. At that time, it was the fastest growing town in the USA.

After half an hour on the Saddle Road which cuts across the northern part of Hawaii, everything changed to a vast, black lava field, sixty miles long. There are wild boar in that area. At nine thousand feet we changed into four wheel drive. At thirteen thousand, within the cinder cone, was Lake Waiau, the second highest in the world next to Lake Titicaca.

Car hire firms prohibit the use of their vehicles from then on as tyres get ripped to shreds. The area is so bleak and rugged that US astronauts tested their moon buggies there because of the terrain's perceived similarity to the surface of the moon. Soon snow was banked at the roadside, again a wonderful blue in its depths..

One year the snow was fifteen feet deep and lay until the fourth of July. There is no lift so the whole area is unspoilt. A road winds conveniently along. So the plan is that you get your kid brother to drop you at the top and then to drive down and collect you at the bottom. Most runs would be about eight hundred yards long but you could go for one and a half miles or more if the snow were deep enough to cover the volcanic outcrops. There is a vast plateau on top and the area was becoming popular with cross country skiers too.

The guide was informative and amusing. Two of our group were paramedics from the Bay area of San Francisco. Whenever we were told anything interesting, they would call out: 'Come on Norma, write it in your little book,' which of course was what I was doing all the time. Often when I look at my notes at the end of each day, I have forgotten most of the details of the morning.

The temperature was 32F with a severe wind chill factor. The wind was seventy-five miles an hour and the snow was blowing sideways. We all got out of the vehicle and strapped on skis. In that ferocious wind, it was difficult to stand, let alone ski. As on Cairngorm, the surface was like white cement. Although the remarkable clarity of the air had been stressed, on this occasion it was almost impossible to see your hand in front of your face. But we all skied, photos were taken and we notched up another success.

We briefly visited the Hawaiian Observatory afterwards. Their eighty-eight inch optical telescope can 'see' four thousand miles into space. We climbed the four flights of steps into the UK observatory and admired the large Infra Red Telescope. We also used the washrooms but that was the extent of our involvement. Our guide referred to possible altitude sickness as the Martini Syndrome. At that height, there is twenty-eight per cent less oxygen than at lower levels.

Soon it was time to head off for my evening flight. Once again the North Star and the Southern Cross were visible in the sky at the same time.

In Waikiki, I was back in the land of palms, hula dancing and grass skirts. In northern Nigeria, I once attempted to make a grass skirt to wear at a fancy dress party. The most pliable grass was 'donkey grass', cut from the roadside. It was a bit too stiff for the purpose. I thought that the effect was quite successful. But when we reached the club someone asked 'What are you? A haystack?'

I checked in at the hotel and had a wonderful Luau (Hawaiian feast) for Mardi Gras in a restaurant on the beach. As I strolled along the sand afterwards, I heard piano music coming from an open verandah. The pianist had trained at the Toronto Conservatory of Music where I had sat rudimentary exams as a child in Toronto in the war.

It was a real 'Red Sails in the Sunset' evening. As the flower-decked outriggers bobbed in the moonlight, I felt that I too could get quite good at this sort of Leisure Time Management.

The Great Wall of China

Chapter Eleven

I have seen dawn and sunset on moors and windy hills
Coming in solemn beauty like slow old tunes of Spain.
Masefield.

That is the story so far. It has been all the more interesting for being unplanned and therefore there have been few disappointments. One thing that I have learnt is that it is no good looking back and having regrets. Two of the saddest words are 'If only.' Often things are taken out of one's hands and the situation cannot be altered. If you can find a solution, or even if one might be possible, the great thing is to try. Failure does not matter. It is important not to be dissuaded by the cold water that others pour onto one's hopes. I have never had the satisfaction of supporting myself by my own efforts. Some will say that I am fortunate and there is no arguing with that.

I always carry rudimentary painting equipment. This led to an article asking 'What do you do if you find yourself alone in the Honeymoon Suite of a hotel in Bermuda?

190

Alone, that is, with a large bottle of champagne and a fabulous view. What do you do if you are drinking in the beauty of St. Basil's Cathedral in Red Square under the gaze of a guardian of Lenin's tomb? What do you do if you are crunching through icebergs in Antarctica or if you are going North to Alaska, with or without John Wayne? One way to capture the atmosphere is to get out your paintbox.' No Victorian traveller would have considered their luggage complete without a travelling paintbox.

It is not necessary to have any particular talent or training in order to paint as you go. A simple, child-like style is all that is needed. A moment can be recorded in this way far more evocatively and personally than with a photograph.

Surprisingly little is needed in the way of equipment for instant art. Start with a pad about the size of a large postcard. Then use a pencil to sketch the outlines. A rubber on the end deals with any mistakes. Then go over the pencil lines with a fine, black, spirit-based fibre pen. A small box of paints and a little brush will allow you to wash in the colours. The kit is completed by a screw-topped bottle of water. I always rinse out the bottle and refill it as soon as I finish painting. This leads to quite an intriguing spin-off. The picture of Montserrat is painted with Bermudan water, the one of Bolivia is painted with water from the samovar on the night train from Moscow to St. Petersburg, the one of Dawson City used water from Raffles…you get the idea.

With this modest equipment you are all set to begin, independent of flat batteries, failed or full memory cards and other hazards of photography. You are also all set to sit down and observe.

Ever since a friend wryly observed: 'The horizon is usually horizontal' I have been conscious that care is needed. Forget about artistic licence, enough will occur without your consciously taking any.

I started this method in Freetown, Sierra Leone. Speed is often important. I was painting outside the prison one day. An observant wag amongst the party of prisoners on fatigues swooped with a cry of 'Oh, ho, an artist!' It was time to pack up swiftly and leave.

Now, carrying paints has become part of travel. It is surprising how quick and unobtrusive you become. Even a short stop is long enough to grab the atmosphere.

There have been interesting sidelines. When painting the Great Wall of China in tooth-juddering cold, I could not think what had gone wrong. Then I realised that the brush had frozen to the paper. My son said that I should have used vodka rather than water. The same happened at minus 25F in the Yukon. In pioneering days there, before thermometers were readily available, temperatures were measured by ingenious means. Various bottles, the contents of which freeze at varying temperatures, were put on the outside windowsills. Quicksilver freezes at minus 40 (this marks the point of parity for Centigrade and Fahrenheit). Coal oil freezes at minus 50F, Jamaica ginger at minus 55F and Perry Davies' painkiller at minus 72F. St John's oil never freezes and that is the day to stay at home. In winter in the Klondike, if you toss the contents of a mug of water into the air at minus 50F, it is ice when it hits the ground. Children there add a few drops of food colouring to the water and see a rainbow as the contents descend.

An unstable world situation has affected travel writing. I was fortunate to hit the market at a time when editors were still accepting freelance pieces as a matter of course. This surprised me even at the time. Every national daily had a considerable staff in its travel section. Why they did not write everything needed in-house was always a mystery, but thank goodness for it.

Travelling the world has made it possible to retrace a lot of steps. A trip to ski in California led to a return to the Queen Mary. The ship is now an hotel anchored off Long Beach, floating in a shallow dock. As I went aboard, the atmosphere was curiously familiar. I had a passenger list which included my family with our cabin numbers.

There was still the same disconcerting metal lip over which to step or trip in order to get into the bathroom. I recognised the black and white chequered tiles on the floor. There was the same choice of sea or fresh water gushing furiously from the giant taps.

My bedroom on the top deck, previously a stateroom, gave a reassuringly unvarying view of Los Angeles. I remembered the wide deck boards, the swimming pool and dining room with its relief map showing the ship's daily progress across the ocean. Now Golden Oldies gather in the afternoons for tea dances; weddings are held there too. As I fell asleep on the first night, the hardly perceptible movement of the ship was an uneasy reminder of that race across the Atlantic and the resultant queasiness.

On board was an American film company making a documentary about such liners, called 'Floating Palaces.' It has since been aired on the Discovery Channel in USA. They were interested to hear about my pre-war voyage and they included me in the film as the only pre-war passenger.

I flew home via New York where I had not been since 1943. On that earlier occasion I had written my name on the wall at the top of the Empire State Building whilst my brother looked on disapprovingly. The wall has been repainted many times since and all graffiti has been removed. I wish that I had been bold enough to etch my name into one of the glass window panes as those signatures are still there and form part of the history of the building.

A week in France making an episode of 'Wish You Were Here' for ITV was another unexpected event in my new life. After my entry was confirmed by Guinness, the programme sent me off to Tignes with a producer, a representative of the host company in the resort, a camera man and sound man. It was a great experience. We needed every moment spent on filming in order eventually to achieve the required twenty minutes on air in the finished production.

A recent press trip made it possible to revisit another milestone in my 1943 wartime journey when I was asked to Philadelphia. Although I spent just a few hours there before we sailed on that Portuguese ship so long ago, the recent visit nevertheless had a maritime flavour. I had by then met Eric Newby who has since died. One of his early books is based on a voyage which he made under sail from Australia to UK, the Great Grain Race. His boat, the Moshulu in which he sailed in 1938, is now based in Philadelphia. I was able to photograph it for him.

A train journey back from Venice on the Orient Express followed another voyage, on MV Orient Express. Sailing from Venice, we made for Athens via the Corinth Canal. The route then took us across the Adriatic and into the Aegean. We were heading for Istanbul. I realised that we would be sailing close to Skiros, where Rupert Brooke was buried in 1915. There were flowers in my cabin so in a gesture to my starry-eyed girlhood, I threw them into the sea, hoping that some would wash up on that shore.

Giving talks recently on a cruise ship gave me the opportunity to revisit Lisbon. The time ashore was brief and I did not get as far as the hotel where we had stayed in 1943. But I found the right area. I was intrigued to pass a neglected doorway, old papers fluttering about in the recess. On the wall, in faded letters, was the word

'Pinkertons.' They were a detective agency and the name rang a faint chord from my wartime visit..

My unbounded optimism caused me to buy a violin when visiting Hong Kong. I had heard a man playing in a restaurant one evening and the poignancy of the music cut straight to my heart. Inspired, I returned to the UK triumphant and had lessons for six months. I was playing it in our cottage one morning and a friend was accompanying me on the piano. A workman was busy in the next room. As he passed by at one point, he grinned and said: 'Oh, I thought you'd got a cat in here.' My teacher, who appears in 'Who's Who in Music' was slightly more encouraging. He paid me one of my life's rare compliments. He said 'You're too good for the Portsmouth Sinfonia, known as the worst orchestra in the world.'

That may sum it all up, really. But it is good enough for me.

When my time came to leave the Bench, I was not too sorry. It was a relief to bow out before I committed some awful gaffe, one which might have attracted headlines in the national press such as 'Woman magistrate asks "What is this world wide web?" or "Who are Posh & Becks?"' It is right that older magistrates retire. No matter how good or experienced, it looks bad if the Bench of three consists only of older people. There are plenty of young, able likelies coming along, with growing families and a sound view of modern life. They have both feet on the ground and an up-to-date knowledge of perils and pitfalls.

It is still important to look for unusual aspects of travel which will appeal to editors. Before I went to Shanghai recently, my son told me that, as well as Tai Chi in the parks in the mornings, there is also ballroom dancing. Leaving the luxury of the Shangri-la Hotel at six am one day, I took a taxi to Fuxing Park. People were strolling along carrying their birds in cages which they hung up on the tree branches. The dancing was about to start. The instructor played suitable music on an old tape recorder and everyone came to life with a Cha Cha Cha.

Encouragement often comes from unexpected quarters, from total strangers in unexpected circumstances.

'I have seen flowers come in stony places
And kind things done by men with ugly faces
And the gold cup won by the worst horse at the races
So I trust too.'

Masefield